Gender, Conflict, and Development

Tsjeard Bouta
Georg Frerks
Ian Bannon

THE WORLD BANK
Washington, D.C.

Photo courtesy of International Committee of the Red Cross

Photographer: Didier Bregnard

Contents

TABLE

Preface

THIS REVIEW IS THE PRODUCT of a collaborative effort between the Conflict Research Unit of the Netherlands Institute of International Relations, "Clingendael," and the World Bank's Conflict Prevention and Reconstruction Unit. The Social Development Team in the Bank's Africa Region supported this publication. The review fills an important gap in the gender, conflict, and development nexus. Although much has been written in academic and policy circles on gender, on conflict, and on the impact of conflict on women, there has been relatively little effort to systematically and comprehensively explore the links with development, particularly in terms of mainstreaming gender in the activities of agencies such as the World Bank, which are supporting countries that are transitioning from conflict to longer-term development.

It has long been argued and accepted that post-conflict reconstruction should not merely recreate past failed structures and systems. Without minimizing the complexities involved, it is clear that countries emerging from the traumatic experience of violent conflict—and the development actors that support them—have an opportunity to do things differently as they set about reversing the damage caused by war and rebuilding more inclusive, accountable, and cohesive societies. Although the window of opportunity is often brief and the reconstruction and transformation invariably a difficult and long-term undertaking, ushering in social change and a more equitable development process must start as soon as the guns are silenced. Gender exclusion undermines the effectiveness of development efforts, even more so in countries that must first rebuild before embarking on the path of sustainable development. Yet the issue of how to engender post-conflict reconstruction has tended to remain on the margins of most policy discussions and donor reconstruction efforts. Part of this marginalization comes from a focus and discourse that sees women primarily as armed conflict victims and not as actors in the conflict, peace, and reconstruction processes. Part also comes from relegating the dialogue on gender imbalances to the advocacy domain, away from that of policy. Without practical policy suggestions on how to address gender in post-conflict reconstruction, opportunities are often missed to increase gender inclusion in the long run. Women have an enormous potential to contribute as empowered actors in the reconstruction and development process.

This review aims to present a more nuanced understanding of gender dynamics in countries that are affected by conflict and, above all, to offer practical policy options that development agencies such as the World Bank can consider in the post-conflict reconstruction and development context. The emphasis is on practical experiences, useful examples, and policy recommendations, which the authors have distilled from an exhaustive literature review, and includes some emerging lessons from the Bank's experience. The review also identifies some important research and analytical gaps. It is hoped that this review will challenge academic and policy researchers to help deepen our understanding of how the international community can effectively support more gender-balanced development in conflict-affected countries.

Steen Lau Jorgensen
Director
Social Development Department

Acknowledgments

As part of the quality assurance procedures of Clingendael's Conflict Research Unit, the authors submitted drafts of this study to a review panel for comments and suggestions. The panel included: Dr. Dorothea Hilhorst, Disaster Studies, Wageningen University; Dr. Dubravka Zarkov, Institute of Social Studies, The Hague; and Ms. Sonja Zimmermann, a gender and development consultant. The World Bank's Conflict Prevention and Reconstruction (CPR) Unit and a number of Bank staff also provided feedback on various drafts. The authors thank the panel members, the CPR Unit, and other Bank staff, (especially Juana Brachet, Florian Fichtel, and Sean Bradley), and consulting editor, Dina Towbin, for their useful suggestions, inputs, and edits. The authors have tried to take all observations, suggestions, and criticisms into consideration in the final report. All errors and omissions are the authors' own.

About the Authors

Tsjeard Bouta is a research fellow at the Netherlands Institute of International Relations, Clingendael, Conflict Research Unit. He is a development sociologist who specializes in conflict studies, with a special research interest in gender and conflict, gender and disarmament, demobilization and reintegration, and democratic governance of the security sector. He was recently involved in research projects on these issues for the Netherlands Ministry of Foreign Affairs, the Netherlands Ministry of Social Affairs and Employment, and Dutch development organizations. His recent publications include: *The Role of SNV (Dutch Development Agency) in Developing Countries in Internal Armed Conflict,* co-authored with Georg Frerks (2001); *Women's Role in Conflict Prevention, Conflict Resolution, and Post-Conflict Reconstruction: Literature Review and Institutional Analysis,* co-authored and co-edited with Georg Frerks (2002); and *Enhancing Democratic Governance of the Security Sector: An Institutional Assessment Framework,* co-authored with Nicolle Ball and Luc van de Goor (2003). He can be reached at: tbouta@clingendael.nl.

Georg Frerks is a rural sociologist with a Ph.D. from Wageningen University in the Netherlands. In the Netherlands Ministry of Foreign Affairs, Dr. Frerks served in several positions at headquarters and abroad. Most recently, he was an evaluator of Dutch international policies and a senior policy advisor to the Ministry's Policy Planning Unit. He is currently head of the Clingendael Conflict Research Unit. He also holds a Special Chair on Conflict Prevention and Conflict Management at Utrecht University and is a professor of disaster studies at Wageningen University's Rural Development Sociology Group. His research interests and publications include: "Evaluation of Humanitarian Assistance in Emergency Situations" (Working Paper

No. 56, *New Issues in Refugee Research*), co-authored with Dorothea Hilhorst (2002); *Mapping Vulnerability: Disasters, Development, and People,* co-edited with Greg Bankoff, and Dorothea Hilhorst (2003); and "Engendering Peace and Conflict" in *Cannons and Canons: Clingendael Views of Global and Regional Politics*, eds. A. van Staden, J. Rood, and H. Labohm, co-authored with Tsjeard Bouta (2003). He can be reached at: gfrerks@clingendael.nl.

Ian Bannon is an economist with an extensive World Bank career, having worked in South Asia, Africa, and Latin America, as well as in the Bank's Policy Research Group. In his last assignment he was the lead economist for Central America; he worked on post-conflict reconstruction in El Salvador, Guatemala, and Nicaragua. Since October 2001, he has been the World Bank's CPR Unit manager in the Social Development Department of the Environmentally and Socially Sustainable Development Network. His policy and research interests include poverty, youth, gender, education, and mental health, especially as they relate to conflict and development. His recent publications include: "Central America: Education Reform in a Post-Conflict Setting: Opportunities and Challenges," (*CPR Working Paper* No. 4), co-authored with J. Marques (2003); *Natural Resources and Violent Conflict: Options and Actions,* co-authored and co-edited with Paul Collier (2003); and *The Role of the World Bank in Conflict and Development: An Evolving Agenda* (2004). He can be reached at: ibannon@worldbank.org.

Abbreviations

BICC	Bonn International Center for Conversion
CDD	Community-driven development
CEDAW	Convention on the Elimination of All Forms of Discrimination Against Women
CPR	Conflict Prevention and Reconstruction
CSO	Civil society organization
DAC	Development Assistance Committee (OECD)
DDR	Disarmament, demobilization, and reintegration
DRC	Democratic Republic of Congo
FAO	Food and Agriculture Organization
FMLN	Farabundo Martí National Liberation Front (El Salvador)
FRP	Feeder Roads Program (Mozambique)
GBV	Gender-based and sexual violence
GTF	Gender Task Force
GTZ	Deutsche Gesellschaft für Technische Zusammenarbeit
HIV/AIDS	Human Immunodeficiency Virus/Acquired Immunity Deficiency Syndrome
ICC	International Criminal Court
ICG	International Crisis Group
ICRC	International Committee of the Red Cross
ICTR	International Criminal Tribunal for Rwanda
ICTY	International Criminal Tribunal for Former Yugoslavia
IDEA	(International) Institute for Democracy and Electoral Assistance
IDP	Internally displaced person

IHL	International Humanitarian Law
ILO	International Labor Organization
IOM	International Office for Migration
IRC	International Rescue Committee
ISS	Institute for Security Studies
KDP	Kecamatan Development Project (Indonesia)
KWI	Kosovo Women's Initiative
LTTE	Liberation Tigers of Tamil Eelam
NGO	Nongovernmental organization
NUPI	Norwegian Institute of International Affairs
OECD	Organisation for Economic Co-operation and Development
OHCHR	Office of the High Commissioner for Human Rights
OSCE	Organization for Security and Economic Cooperation in Europe
PRIO/Uppsala	International Peace Research Institute of Oslo, Norway, and the University of Uppsala, Sweden
RUF	Revolutionary United Front (Sierra Leone)
SIDA	Swedish International Development Agency
SNV	Dutch Development Agency
STD	Sexually transmitted disease
SP GTF	Gender Task Force of the Stability Pact for Southeastern Europe
UN	United Nations
UNCHS	UN Center for Human Settlements
UNDDA	UN Department for Disarmament Affairs
UNDESA	UN Department of Economic and Social Affairs
UNDG	UN Development Group
UNDP	UN Development Programme
UNESC	UN Economic and Social Council
UNFPA	UN Fund for Population Activities
UNHCR	UN High Commissioner for Refugees
UNICEF	UN Children's Fund
UNIFEM	UN Development Fund for Women
UNMIK	UN Mission in Kosovo
UNSC	UN Security Council
UNSG	UN Secretary-General
UNTAC	UN Transitional Authority in Cambodia
USAID	United States Agency for International Development
WCRWC	Women's Commission for Refugee Women and Children
WHO	World Health Organization
WSP	War-Torn Societies Project

Executive Summary

Introduction

THIS REVIEW ADDRESSES the gender dimensions of intrastate conflict. It is organized around eight areas or themes that are related to the World Bank's agenda on gender, conflict, and development: (i) gender and warfare; (ii) gender and sexual violence; (iii) gender and formal peace processes; (iv) gender and informal peace processes; (v) gender and the post-conflict legal framework; (vi) gender and work; (vii) gender and rehabilitating social services; and (viii) gender and community-driven development. For each theme, the authors have analyzed the gender-specific roles of women and men before, during, and after conflict, the gender role changes throughout conflict, the development challenges in sustaining positive gender role changes and mitigating negative effects, and the policy options for addressing these gender roles, dynamics, and challenges. The suggested policy options are intended to be gender- as well as conflict-sensitive, and ideally should contribute to more equal gender relations. The relevance and applicability of the policy options are identified and key considerations outlined that the Bank would need to take into account in assessing policy options. Finally, further research areas are suggested on the gender, conflict, and development nexus.

This review is based on the authors' desk study of more than 230 secondary resources. Because of the nature of the sources consulted, the study is slightly biased toward the post-conflict phase and women's roles relative to men's, and toward qualitative rather than quantitative or comparative data that would allow for generalized conclusions. Nevertheless, the authors believe that the reviewed material provides a sufficient basis for the analysis, options, and recommendations.

Gender and Warfare

Women play many *roles in warfare*. They can be combatants—fighting in recognized military institutions (such as regular armies) and with nonstate military actors (such as guerrilla forces)—and/or work as cooks, porters, administrators, spies, partners, and sex slaves. Women also support warfare as civilians, for example, by broadcasting hate speech and instilling hatred of enemy groups in new generations, thus contributing to the militarization of men and society. In addition, women can be male soldier supporters or their dependents. Many abducted women are among the dependents; they have been forced to marry or become an army commander's partner. In practice, women usually combine their roles; they are fighters, cooks, and mothers concurrently.

One of the *gender-specific roles* in warfare relates to motives for joining the army. Whereas women and men can become soldiers for similar reasons, many women do so to obtain more rights and gender equality. They are also deliberately recruited to add legitimacy or symbolic power to the war effort. However, many women, like numerous men and boys, are forced to join against their will, abducted into combat, or forced to become sexual and domestic slaves.

A major *change* in gender relations is the tendency toward more equal gender relations in fighting forces as compared to the pre- and post-conflict phases. While gender roles may be more equal in armies, where women benefit from new opportunities, this is generally more than offset by negative effects such as sexual violence.

A *key development challenge* is to acknowledge both women's and men's participation in armies and to provide assistance to *all* women that joined the armies—with or without weapons. This assistance should not be provided exclusively through disarmament, demobilization, and reintegration (DDR) programs. Rather the implementation of reintegration activities should be in parallel with disarmament and demobilization activities—to avoid women's self-demobilization.

Suggested *policy options* for security and reintegration agencies are: to recast the definition of female combatants in such a way that it includes women who are part of (ir)regular armies in any capacity; to make extra efforts to track and identify women in armies so they are included in post-conflict assistance programs; to target women in support roles and/or abducted women separately from their husbands and male counterparts; and to inform female ex-soldiers of their legal rights and how to access DDR programs.

Rehabilitation agencies should anticipate the different economic, social, and psychological needs and opportunities of female ex-soldiers. Psychological support needs should consider issues that have a greater impact on women, their more difficult social reintegration, and their exposure to gender-based and sexual violence in and after conflict.

Gender-Based and Sexual Violence

Gender-based and sexual violence (GBV) is defined in this book as physical, sexual, and psychological violence against both women and men that occurs in the family and the community and is perpetrated or condoned by the state. In conflict situations, GBV is committed against civilians and soldiers. It is not an accidental side effect of war, but a crime against the individual and an act of aggression against the entire community or nation.

Regarding *gender-specific roles* related to GBV, women are more vulnerable to GBV than men because of prevailing oppressive gender relations, particularly in conflict situations. The trafficking in and sexual exploitation of human beings, particularly of women, tends to increase in conflict situations. Many women engage in prostitution to survive conflict; sex also becomes a form of bargaining power. Widespread GBV during conflict increases the spread of sexually transmitted diseases (STDs) such as HIV/AIDS, especially among women.

One of the *changes* in GBV relates to its intensity during conflict. GBV increases and often becomes an accepted practice during conflict and in the post-conflict phase. With the transition from conflict to peace, a shift in GBV seems to take place from the public to the private domain through an increase in domestic violence.

A major *development challenge* is to support the protection and recovery of GBV survivors. This could best be done via a multidimensional approach that actively involves GBV survivors, both male and female, their communities, the health sector, social services, and the legal and security sectors.

Key GBV *policy options* are to target both men and women and to raise awareness to ensure that GBV in conflict is addressed in post-conflict reconstruction. Other options are to strengthen both medical assistance for GBV survivors and local capacity to provide psychological counseling to all the actors involved, while assessing its potentially different impacts on female and male GBV survivors. Agencies should ensure that women and men have similar protection against GBV, the same information on and access to GBV medical services, and are assisted by a same-sex health worker (and translator) for their medical examination. They should encourage the legal protection of women and men against GBV through existing laws and newly adopted legislation and build institutional capacity among the police, judiciary, border guards, and social services.

Gender and Formal Peace Processes

Most political institutions in conflict and nonconflict societies tend to perpetuate an exclusionary attitude and culture toward women. As a result, compared to men relatively few women become involved in formal peace processes during and after conflict. Beyond this quantitative *difference,* there is a qualitative difference; women are likely to make a different contribution to the peace process. Their increased participation may generate wider public support for peace accords.

Regarding gender-role *changes,* additional analysis is needed to determine whether women's participation in formal political processes increases during conflict. Since prevailing social structures and gender divisions tend to accompany the return of peace, many women have to retreat from political and public life. However, this dip in female participation may be temporary and is often reversed due to external pressure to establish democratic systems and open political space for women.

The *key development challenge* is to use the post-conflict momentum to focus attention on gender-equality issues and to increase the involvement of women and other marginalized groups in the peace process.

To incorporate gender equality into peace accords, policy options include: organizing training and information-sharing events for politicians or those involved in the peace talks; developing wider processes of political consultation or representation, for example, with women's organizations; increasing the number of female politicians by training women to run for political office; fostering discussions within public and political bodies about women's involvement; setting legislative or party quotas to ensure a minimum number of female politicians; and establishing indicators to assess the influence of female and male politicians on political outcomes and on the political culture and process.

Gender, Informal Peace Processes, and Rebuilding Civil Society

Informal peace processes are usually complementary to formal peace processes, but are not limited to them. The main *gender difference* is that more women than men tend to become active in informal processes.

An important *gender-role change* is that conflict offers many women the opportunity to enter informal peace processes. Many individual women and women's civil society organizations (CSOs) in conflict have assumed the roles and tasks of public institutions, undertaken relief work, channeled international assistance to recipients, lobbied to incorporate rights and specific provisions in peace accords, and encouraged women to participate in elections. The *key development challenge* is to support these women and women's CSOs (also men and men's CSOs), not only during but also after conflict. They can form the foundation for a strong and more inclusive civil and political post-conflict society, which is essential to effective, sustainable, and more inclusive reconstruction and development efforts.

Policy options include: strengthening the capacity of individual women and women's CSOs to bridge the gap between informal and formal peace processes; encouraging and training men and women in informal peace processes to make the shift toward formal processes; and involving individual women and women's CSOs actively in post-conflict rehabilitation and reconstruction. Community-driven reconstruction approaches can provide a unique opportunity to engage local women and men in kick-starting the local reconstruction process and helping to bridge the divide between crisis and development. International agencies can also assist in restructuring, professionalizing, and providing longer-term support to women's CSOs.

Gender-Sensitizing the Post-Conflict Legal Framework

Conflict societies often have an opportunity to undergo a transformation in the security, political, and socioeconomic realms that is usually accompanied by constitutional and legal reforms. From a *gender perspective,* these reforms are the moment to enshrine gender-equality issues and other basic human rights in the constitution and to formalize women's and men's democratic representation and participation in all decisionmaking structures of the government and society at large. Furthermore, the transition period provides the momentum to restore justice and accountability mechanisms and to reestablish the rule of law. In this context, judicial mechanisms need to focus on *gender-specific issues* such as reparations and rehabilitation policies, compensation for human rights violations, and GBV issues, such as rape and other forms of sexual violence.

Key challenges include extending gender equality provisions to nonstatutory and customary law, ensuring that effective implementation mechanisms are developed, and building judicial mechanisms that do not marginalize women's experiences and do not consider women only as victims, but also as perpetrators of violence in conflict settings.

Supporting governments—through awareness-raising and information campaigns—to ratify, respect, and implement relevant international standards would be a first *policy option* to ensure women's and men's rights in conflict situations. Other options include developing and enforcing gender-sensitive legislation at the national level, informing and training women and men on their rights, and encouraging the judiciary to enforce gender-sensitive laws.

With regard to judicial mechanisms, a central *policy option* is to encourage them to acknowledge, condemn, and prosecute all crimes committed *by* women and men *against* women and men in conflict situations.

Gender and Work: Creating Equal Labor Market Opportunities

The scope of gender and work covers the relationship between gender and agricultural work, informal urban work, and formal urban work. Regarding *gender-specific differences and gender role changes* in relation to work during conflict, many women take on tasks that their husbands or other male relatives had done previously. At the same time, displacement and post-conflict unemployment undermine men's sense of identity as providers, which, in turn, often translates into anti-social behavior and violence directed at women. In the *agricultural sector,* women may take over responsibility for working the land, caring for livestock, trading, or carrying out wage labor outside the home. The key problem is that women are often denied access to, owning, and inheriting productive resources in their own names. In urban areas, a kind of "feminization" of the *informal sector* takes place during conflict. Women may regard work in the informal sector as a way of liberation and empowerment or as a means of exploitation and survival. Regarding the *formal sector,* key gender differences relate to unequal promotion opportunities, remuneration, rights, and so on for women and men. Yet the net effect during or after conflict is not clear as women are both discouraged and encouraged to take up formal employment.

The major *development challenge* is to take advantage of and assist in sustaining positive gender role changes regarding work as a result of conflict by designing economic assistance programs that build on newly acquired skills and encouraging women and men to continue in their new activities.

One important contribution would be to try to reduce women's domestic and reproductive burdens, so that women who want to earn a living outside the home could do so. This should go hand-in-hand with efforts to reform gender-biased labor laws and raise awareness on gender equality issues in the workplace. In relation to informal urban employment, microcredit schemes have brought many women much-needed relief, but their economic sustainability and empowerment potential are often limited, so they should be complemented by other forms of support. Vocational training programs can be useful if they are based on sound market research and gender analysis and adapted to women's and men's different skills and needs. The formal sectors that traditionally employ women can be an important source of employment, but women can also be supported to apply new skills and experience gained during conflict. Greater labor equality can also help over the long run.

Gender and Rehabilitating Social Services

In most conflict situations, *gender-specific roles* dictate that women become the primary home providers of health care and education. While women's regular household tasks become more complex during conflict, they often also become responsible for providing health care to ill, old, and injured family and community members. In addition, some women also provide childcare and home schooling for their children during conflict. On the one hand, this key *gender role change* considerably increases women's burden of dependency, but it may also strengthen women's capacities and organizational capabilities, inducing them to take on more public roles during or after conflict.

From a development perspective, the first *key challenge* is to try to keep health and education facilities functioning during conflict; the post-conflict challenge is to restore and reshift these services from the private to the public domain quickly. Another challenge is to further gender-sensitize post-conflict education and health services.

Although conflict's overall impact on education systems is unambiguously negative, the post-conflict period presents a good opportunity to gender-sensitize the education system. This window of opportunity, however, tends to be brief as education systems can recover very quickly, and vested interests and pre-conflict social norms are also quickly reestablished.

Reshifting education and health care services in a post-conflict society may take a long time. One policy option for this transformation phase is to start changing the perception that men's and particularly women's health and education work are a natural extension of domestic work and not a professional occupation. Another policy option is to support community- and home-based schooling and health care facilities, where usually many women are involved, as a first step toward reconstructing formal systems. Further options can help gender-sensitize health systems through reproductive health care and psychological assistance to conflict survivors, by treating war-induced handicaps and disabilities, GBV, and other post-conflict traumatic disorders, and by providing STD and HIV/AIDS prevention and treatment. To gender-sensitize education, agencies could pay more attention to adult education, particularly for women, and to girls' high dropout rates from school during and after conflict. Finally, they could support the development of nondiscriminatory education and training.

Gender and Community-Driven Development

Rebuilding social capital and cohesion are deeply *gendered* processes, even though they are still described in a nongendered manner. Post-conflict development efforts increasingly emphasize participatory and community-driven development processes to strengthen social cohesion and build bridging social capital. A major potential *change* is that the adoption of community-driven approaches to post-conflict reconstruction can encourage more gender-balanced representation in local decisionmaking processes and, if sustained, provide a springboard for greater women's empowerment and involvement in broader political processes.

A *key development challenge* is to address factors that constrain women's participation in local community development efforts and their representation in decisionmaking structures and processes. *Policy options* include adopting community-based approaches in reconstruction, mobilizing the support of men and the community to support women's participation, investing in training community leaders and gender facilitators, adapting timing and logistics to women's needs, and ensuring strong monitoring and evaluation.

Policy Options

Policy options primarily relate to the Bank's mandate and agenda, but they may be used by other agencies working in the post-conflict reconstruction and development nexus. The options focus on longer-term development challenges and explicitly go beyond the notion of women and men as only conflict victims. While policy options are offered to try to ensure and sustain more balanced gender relations in conflict-affected societies, there is no substitute for context-specific analysis—for an assessment of reality on the ground and the country-specific scope for policy reforms and options.

To enhance implementation of the suggested policy options, a number of intra-organizational requirements are outlined that an institution such as the World Bank should consider. They relate to the need to develop concrete gender and armed conflict policies, to translate these policies into action plans and benchmarks, to monitor and evaluate gender- and conflict-related activities to assess their impact on gender roles and relationships in conflict, to sensitize and train staff, and to incorporate gender and conflict issues into existing programs, projects, tools, and instruments. Four other relevant issues are also discussed: objectives to be set, timing of interventions, interventions' target groups, and other challenges.

Issues for Further Analysis in Gender, Conflict, and Development

Despite increased attention to the gender, conflict, and development nexus, major analytical gaps remain. As a first conceptual point, a more comprehensive gender focus needs to be adopted beyond reductionist perspectives on women's roles. As a second conceptual point, there is the need for engendering conflict analysis; most analytical and policy models, approaches, tools, instruments, and conflict checklists lack a gender-specific theoretical and operational basis. This applies to the field of early warning and early response, conflict prevention, conflict monitoring, and the evaluation of conflict-related policies as well as the emerging fields of conflict analysis and Peace and Conflict Impact Assessments. Incorporating a gender perspective and suggesting modifications, where appropriate, should be considered.

Further specific analysis is required on: certain gender role changes; the policy implications of the concepts of masculinity and femininity; the link between masculinity and violence; the theme of child soldiers; the relative importance of gender as compared to other identity markers in shaping women's and men's roles and relationships in conflict-affected areas; the gender dimensions of macroeconomic policies; the ways to link existing insights in the fields of gender, conflict, and development cooperation; the gender dimensions of the concepts of social capital and social cohesion; and on the need for more transformative approaches that can fundamentally alter the balance of power in gender relations as societies rebuild after conflict.

CHAPTER I

Introduction

THIS REVIEW LARGELY FOCUSES on areas that are related to the World Bank's agenda on gender, conflict, and development. While the Bank may not be active in all the areas that the review covers, it often plays a leading role in post-conflict reconstruction, and these are areas that need to be taken into account in the design and implementation of development strategies in conflict-affected countries. The review pays no or little attention to issues outside the Bank's mandate, such as humanitarian aid, disarmament, and control of small arms. However, it does include issues that may not be directly linked to the Bank's mandate, such as political reforms and peace negotiations, but which are clearly related to areas broadly within the Bank's mandate, such as institutional reform, governance, and the rule of law. They are also highly relevant areas in terms of a more comprehensive approach to post-conflict reconstruction, including the need to ensure citizen security and protection, especially that of women, against post-conflict violence. These issues should inform the Bank's development efforts in post-conflict countries.

This review is based on secondary material, including academic and policy documents. Although the authors examined more than 230 sources, there may be other important material that could have contributed to the study. Nonetheless, the authors believe that the review covers the major trends in contemporary literature. The authors selected the material to be reviewed based on the following criteria. Sources had to:

- Directly focus on the gender, conflict, and development nexus, with only limited reference to numerous other sources on conflict and feminist studies;[1]
- Be written in English, almost exclusively;
- Be written in the last five years in view of the field's dynamic and evolving nature; and
- Be relevant in terms of development policy formulation or implementation.

Objectives and Focus

In the mid-1990s, the gender dimensions of peace and conflict started to appear on international policy agendas. Two milestones were the Beijing Declaration and Platform for Action (1995) and United Nations (UN) Security Council Resolution 1325 on Women, Peace and Security (UN Security Council 2000). Both stressed the importance of women's equal participation and their full involvement in the maintenance and promotion of peace and security, as well as the need to increase women's role in decision-making in conflict prevention and resolution, and post-conflict reconstruction.[2] Although it is now well accepted that women and men are affected by and respond to conflict differently, and that gender relations change substantially as a result of conflict, development actors have had difficulty translating this information into practical policies and sustaining positive changes in gender roles and relationships in the post-conflict period. Few agencies working in conflict address comprehensively and systematically conflict's gender dimensions. Agencies tend to concentrate on the post-conflict phase and give less attention to gender relations before and during conflict. Furthermore, many organizations tend to focus only on certain roles of women and men in conflict, while some tend to oversimplify reality, for example, by describing men in a stereotypical way as aggressors and women as peacemakers. Similarly, women's role as victims is often emphasized at the expense of other roles they can and do play. Many agencies do not fully recognize the multifaceted and dynamic roles of women and men in conflict situations.

This review depicts women's and men's roles in conflict, analyzes differences and changes in these roles and ensuing gender relations, and assesses the sustainability of such changes. The challenges of these differences and changes for development are outlined. Policy options are provided for a development agency such as the World Bank to address these gender roles, dynamics, and challenges. Suggested policy options are intended to be gender- as well as conflict-sensitive, and ideally should contribute to more equal gender relations. The review closes with suggested areas for further research.

Terminology and Concepts

While the review does not enter into definitional or academic debates on major concepts, such as intrastate conflict, gender, gender equality, and mainstreaming, the authors have indicated how key terms are used in this review.

The study's primary focus is on *intrastate conflict*, less so on interstate conflict, although the latter may generate lessons as it also impacts on gender relations. Intrastate conflict was selected based on the World Bank CPR Unit's focus areas and reflects the fact that most conflicts over the last 15 years can be classified as intrastate conflicts. Intrastate conflict does not concern a (declared) war between two different states, but is characterized by the fact that the conflict's major causes and protagonists can be found mainly within a particular society. Yet it should be underlined that in terms of support, funding, and attempts to deal with it, intrastate conflict usually involves external actors. Therefore, the term is misleading to some degree. Except for the use of violence *per se,* some form of organized combat and a planned systematic strategy further characterize intrastate conflict. Intrastate conflict excludes spontaneous uprisings of short duration, unique or singular skirmishes such as sporadic riots and *coups d'état,* or crime.

Gender refers to the socially constructed roles ascribed to women and men, as opposed to biological and physical characteristics. Gender roles vary according to socioeconomic, political, and cultural contexts, and are affected by other factors, including age, class, and ethnicity. Gender roles are learned and negotiated, or contested. They are therefore changeable. Besides differences in roles *between* women and men, roles *among* women and men differ as well, while both women and men may also combine different roles individually over time or even simultaneously. Although women are seen as victims in general in conflict situations, they are often mothers, breadwinners, combatants, or peace activists as well. In addition, making gender synonymous with the positions and roles of women and men still constitutes an extremely limiting and reductionist gender view. As Dubravka Zarkov wrote in a communication to the authors:

> Gender is an organizing principle of social life that affects different levels of social reality, not only individual people. The level of individual (subjective) identities (of which we accept, or resist and negotiate identification with specific notions of femininity and masculinity) is only one of the levels on which gender operates. This is also the level in which individuals assume (or refuse or negotiate) specific gender roles. Narrowing the meaning of gender to individual women and men and their gender roles excludes other levels on which gender operates: the level of institutions and organizations producing specific masculinities and femininities, and at the same time being the product of gender; the level of ideology and doctrine, with their (gendered) values and norms; finally, the symbolic level (not only female and male bodies as symbols of nations and states, or victims or heroes, but also meanings that are—at first sight—not seen as gender, such as sovereignty). Furthermore, processes are gendered (based on specific gendered assumptions) and

they gender reality and so does development. This gendered or gendering terminology actually indicates that gender does not exist outside
other social relations of power.

In this connection, gender relations cut across other social factors and
processes based on, for example, class, age, and ethnicity, each of which
may have gendered qualities. The authors recognize the multi-layered
and interconnected nature of gender and gendering levels. However,
most of the literature reviewed was restricted to roles and individual
identities. Only in rare cases were institutional, ideological, and symbolic levels touched on or how processes tend to 'gender reality'
discussed.[3] Notwithstanding the relevance of those issues, the authors
could only conclude that further work on them is needed. In practice,
this means that in this study, analysis was restricted by necessity mainly
to the level of gender roles, gender relationships, and their dynamics
with an unavoidable emphasis on women, as explained below.

The review tries to take a *dynamic perspective*. It aims to understand the interplay between conflict processes and gender roles by
focusing on the resulting changes. Although conflict and gender relations mutually reinforce each other—gender roles adapt individuals in
war roles, and war roles provide the context within which individuals
are socialized into gender roles (Goldstein 2001)—this review emphasizes how women and men acquire and consolidate new identities and
roles in conflict situations.

Most literature studied for this review tended to focus only on
women in conflict, even though references often claim to present a
broader gender focus. This tendency is pervasive and affects the
authors' ability to present a balanced and truly gendered analysis.[4]
There is, of course, literature dealing with nonspecified, presumably
male, actors in conflict, but these are not approached in a gender-
specific way, and therefore do not add to the understanding of the problem set out in this report. Consequently, the review has not generated as
much information on men as on women in conflict. This undermines
part of the first study objective, namely, to depict men's key roles and
the nature of and changes in gender relationships. Similarly, to a certain
degree this affects the comprehensive nature of the suggested policy implications and policy options. These issues point to the need to conduct
further systematic studies on men and gender relations in conflict.

The same is obviously true for *masculinities,* which is understood
as the social and historical construction of male gender. In this connection, the role of masculinized institutions (the army, businesses,
and the bureaucracy—where masculine traits are prized[5]) requires attention in the same manner as the earlier-mentioned institutionalized
forms of gender. To the degree that the authors have come across

relevant references, these were included in the review. Most of the literature encountered on this topic had little direct policy focus.

Gender equality relates to the equal rights, responsibilities, and opportunities of women, men, girls, and boys. It is often regarded as a human rights issue and considered a precondition for and indication of sustainable, people-centered development. A recent World Bank (2001b) report distinguishes equality under the law, equality of opportunity (equality of rewards for work and equality in access to human capital and other productive resources that enable opportunity), and equality of voice (the ability to influence and contribute to the development process). It is likely that without a clear gender equality focus, interventions will fail to capitalize on opportunities to decrease disparities between women and men and to build on their potential to sustain peace and development.

Gender mainstreaming is seen as the process of assessing the implications for women and men of any planned action, including legislation, policies, or programs in all areas and at all levels. It is a strategy for making women's as well as men's concerns and experiences an integral dimension of the design, implementation, monitoring, and evaluation of policies and programs in all political, economic, and societal spheres, so that women and men benefit equally and inequality is not perpetuated [UN Economic and Social Council (UNESC) 1997]. This usually involves considering special measures to improve women's access to decisionmaking, services, and resources.

Finally, women and men are regarded as *social actors*. An actor approach takes as its departure point the differentiated interests, characteristics, and activities of the individuals involved. Thus, these operate on the basis of multiple and contested realities and not as a homogeneous group. An actor orientation recognizes the centrality of human agency as actively involved in the production and reproduction of the social world.[6] It underlines how interests, knowledge, and power are contested and negotiated in everyday practice. Actors accord meaning to and interpret what happens, thus shaping their own responses on the basis of their understanding, capacities, and resources. While on the one hand they may be forced by the conditions of conflict into certain positions, on the other hand, they will try to deliberately change their roles according to their own agendas and strategies. It is self-evident that the issue of gender plays an important role in such a perspective. Actor orientation also implies a particular understanding of livelihoods and development interventions as "materialized and socially constructed through the interplay, contestation and negotiation of values and interests within specific domains and arenas of social action" (Long 1997). It juxtaposes mechanistic ideas about linear

policy implementation by focusing on the "reinterpretation or transformation of policy during the implementation process, such that
there is in fact no straight line from policy to outcomes" (Long and
van der Ploeg 1989). An actor orientation's strength is that it avoids
viewing women and men as "structural or cultural dopes" and tries to
see how individuals create room for maneuver. Like feminist analyses
of power, the actor approach tries to avoid associating women with
victimization and vulnerability. Overemphasizing this approach, however, could lead to a failure to see how gender relations are institutionalized and embedded in persistent cultural, religious, legal, and
other structures. According to Dubravka Zarkov, the actor approach
may risk an "individualization" of power relations that dwells in
social structures, values, ideologies, and relations through an assumption of a choice, where this choice does not exist effectively.

The Bank's Approach to Gender and Conflict

Since the 1980s, the World Bank has made progress in *integrating gender issues* into country work and lending. Several organizational
changes were made to facilitate greater attention to gender and development issues, including issuing an Operational Policy on the gender
dimension of development in 1994, and creating a Gender and Development Board in 1997. Recognizing the need to find more effective
ways to integrate gender-responsive actions into the Bank's development assistance, in September 2001, the Board of Executive Directors
endorsed a mainstreaming gender strategy (World Bank 2002). The
World Bank Policy Research Report that preceded the mainstreaming
strategy (World Bank 2001b) argues that on one level, poverty exacer-
bates gender disparities, while on another level gender inequalities hin-
der development. A central message is that ignoring gender disparities
comes at great cost—to people's well-being and to countries' ability to
grow sustainably, to govern effectively, and thus to reduce poverty.
The report argues for a three-part strategy to promote gender equality:

- Reform institutions to establish equal rights and opportunities
  for women and men;
- Foster economic development to strengthen incentives for more
  equal resources and participation; and
- Take active measures to redress persistent disparities in command
  over resources and political voice.

Although the Bank's mainstreaming gender strategy in its work
presents a comprehensive set of actions and recommendations, it does
not address the particular challenges (and opportunities) posed by

countries that are affected by conflict or are embarking on donor-supported post-conflict reconstruction processes.

The adoption of a more systematic and comprehensive approach to *conflict and development* has been a more recent development in the World Bank. Following experiences in the West Bank and Gaza and in Bosnia and Herzegovina, in 1997, the Bank defined its approach to post-conflict reconstruction and created a small Post-Conflict Unit. However, in the late 1990s, the Bank sought to redefine its conflict role more comprehensively, from one focused on physical reconstruction to one that emphasized greater sensitivity to conflict in Bank activities. The approach was reflected in a new Operational Policy on development cooperation and conflict (World Bank 2001, 2001a) that the Board of Executive Directors approved in January 2001; to signal this change in approach, the Post-Conflict Unit was renamed the Conflict Prevention and Reconstruction Unit (CPR 2004c). As the Bank attempted to mainstream greater sensitivity to conflict in its work, it became clear that gender was an important missing dimension and did not figure systematically in its conflict work; conversely, rarely if at all did conflict figure in the gender mainstreaming agenda. This review aims to begin to fill this important gap.

Limitations

The review was subject to a number of limitations:

- It could not cover all possibly relevant literature in view of resource constraints.
- The literature reviewed showed a certain bias in that it tended to be based on the experiences of agencies involved in conflict settings. This was compounded by the predominance of reports emanating from larger multilateral agencies and international nongovernmental organizations (NGOs) as compared to grassroots civil society organizations (CSOs). The authors feel that more in-depth material might have been available at the field level, but they were not in a position to interview women and men directly regarding their experiences. The Panos oral testimony project and the resulting book, *Arms to Fight, Arms to Protect,* however, provides the testimony of 85 women and can complement the policy and academic studies discussed in this report (Bennett, Bexley, and Warnock 1995).
- The publications' quality varied or was difficult to judge. The authors accept the literature findings at face value, apart from mentioning limitations discussed by the sources themselves.

- Many of the challenges and policy options to engender the development process in conflict-affected countries are also challenges in stable settings. Where possible, the review attempts to highlight the ways in which conflict impacts gender relations, while recognizing that in some cases the gender challenges are not dissimilar from those in countries not affected by conflict, although they are exacerbated and made more complex by conflict.
- The review focuses largely on the post-conflict phase, reflecting the fact that the link between gender, conflict, and development usually receives more attention after the conflict has ended.
- There were certain omissions in the literature reviewed. Some issues, such as men's involvement in informal politics, women's participation in formal politics during conflict, and women's engagement in the formal labor market during and after conflict, tended to receive little attention or were dealt with in a fragmented or anecdotal manner. This made it difficult to ascertain whether issues or trends identified in the literature were time- or context-specific or had broader relevance. Whenever possible, the authors indicate the context from which the material is taken or present interesting examples in text boxes.
- There is relatively little quantitative or comparative work on which to base generalized conclusions; therefore some modesty in drawing general inferences from this report is justified. Nonetheless, the authors believe that the material reviewed provides sufficient basis for the options and recommendations presented.

The Links among Gender, Conflict, and Development

The following chapters highlight the major gender dimensions of conflict and are organized around eight major interlinked areas or themes: (i) gender and warfare; (ii) gender-based and sexual violence; (iii) gender and formal peace processes; (iv) gender and informal peace processes; (v) gender and the post-conflict legal framework; (vi) gender and work; (vii) gender and rehabilitating social services; and (viii) gender and community-driven development. Each thematic area begins with a brief introduction that sets the context, followed by a discussion of how conflict affects the gender-specific roles of women and men. Rather than assume a priori that women's and men's roles are intrinsically different, or that there are no important differences, the authors have analyzed differences in their roles and how gender roles and gender relations change as a result of conflict. Development challenges and proposed policy options are identified. Where available, lessons learned and best practices are provided.

CHAPTER 2

Gender and Warfare: Female Combatants and Soldiers' Wives

Overview

THERE IS INCREASING EVIDENCE and recognition that women are actively involved in fighting during conflict. Although female participation varies widely in military institutions authorized to use force, such as in regular armies, and in nonstate military actors, such as in irregular armies, they tend to represent between 10 percent and one-third of both these types of forces. Besides combat roles, female soldiers can be cooks, porters, administrators, doctors, spies, partners, and sex slaves for male soldiers. Women also support warfare as civilians, for example, by broadcasting hate speech and instilling hatred against enemy groups in new generations, and thus contributing to the militarization of men and society.

Key development challenges are to acknowledge women's and men's participation in armies and to target *all* women that joined the armies—with or without weapons—with assistance. This assistance should not be provided exclusively through DDR programs. In a number of examples, DDR programs have not targeted women or have only targeted women with weapons, thus excluding women who could not hand in a weapon at disarmament camps, and have not always managed to adequately identify women that were eligible for assistance. As a result, a large number of women never actually enter the DDR program and are self-demobilized. There is thus a need to further improve DDR and rehabilitation programs. One suggestion is to establish a clearer *division of labor between security agencies and reintegration or rehabilitation agencies*. Security agencies generally target women with weapons—and sometimes female dependents of armed male combatants—with disarmament and demobilization assistance, whereas rehabilitation agencies aim to reach all women that joined the armies with reintegration support, often combined with broader assistance projects focused on communities as a whole. However, this division of labor is only effective if security and reintegration agencies have clear mandates and effective coordination mechanisms. This includes the early identification of women in armies, the protection of women in all activities, appropriate funding of disarmament and demobilization as compared to reintegration activities, and the adequate timing of reintegration activities—i.e., the implementation of reintegration activities in parallel with disarmament and demobilization activities, sequenced with disarmament and demobilization activities—to avoid women's self-demobilization.

Suggested *policy options* for security and reintegration agencies are to recast the definition of female combatants so that it includes women who are part of (ir)regular armies in any capacity, including but not limited to women in support roles, and women forced to provide sexual services. Another policy option is to make extra efforts to track and identify women in armies so that they do not remain under-reported and thus excluded from post-conflict assistance programs. It is also vital to target women in support roles and/or abducted women separately from their husbands and male counterparts. Moreover, extra efforts are required to inform female ex-soldiers on access to DDR programs, for example, by disseminating information via women-centered communication channels such as health centers, food distribution points, churches, and schools.

For security agencies and to a lesser extent rehabilitation agencies, the demobilization phase can be used to inform ex-soldiers about their legal rights in civilian life, but also to help them to enter into new forms of social organization such as veterans' groups and women's organizations. These newly established frameworks for concerted action could help avoid isolation and encourage reintegration, particularly of female ex-soldiers. It is also important to examine whether and how demobilization activities and facilities could be made more gender-sensitive and more responsive to local needs and circumstances.

Rehabilitation agencies should anticipate the different economic, social, and psychological needs and opportunities of all female ex-soldiers. Regardless of the extent to which rehabilitation agencies link these efforts to broader community-based recovery programs, female ex-soldiers must be assisted in dealing with a range of issues. These can include the women's return to prevailing labor divisions, their inability to own and inherit land, and their restricted mobility due to their domestic burdens. Efforts that encourage their social reintegration may need to focus on the fact that female ex-soldiers usually have to retake their earlier family roles, which are strikingly different from their wartime experiences, and the fact that they are often accused of sexual promiscuity during conflict and face exclusion and ostracism. Finally, psychological support needs to consider issues that have a greater impact on women, their more difficult social reintegration, and their exposure to gender-based and sexual violence in and after conflict.

This chapter looks at the role of men and women in warfare, while other chapters focus on their engagement in non-war activities, recognizing that most women and men do not fight and continue with their normal daily activities (Anderson 1999).

Women in Conflict

It is usually assumed that, in comparison to each other, men are more violent and women are more peaceful. Fukuyama (1998), for example, refers to neo-Darwinist research to suggest that males are genetically predisposed to violence. Hilhorst and Frerks (1999) take a more constructivist approach, arguing that gender differences are context-specific and determined by each situation. In reviewing the case of Sierra Leone, Mazurana and Carlson (2004) conclude that women and girls in the fighting forces had a complex experience—they were captives and dependents, but they were also involved in planning and executing the war. Powley (2003) also points out that a small minority of women (2.3 percent of genocide suspects) were involved in perpetrating Rwanda's violence. Whatever the differences between these approaches, women's active participation in conflicts is widely acknowledged.[7] For instance, female combatants have been active in Algeria, El Salvador, Eritrea, Ethiopia, Mozambique, Namibia, Nepal, Nicaragua, South Africa, Sri Lanka, and Zimbabwe.[8] McKay and Mazurana (2004) collected data on girls' involvement in fighting forces during 1990–2003. They found that girls were part of fighting forces in 55 countries and were involved in armed conflict in 38 of the 55 countries, all of them internal conflicts. In addition, girls in fighting forces participated in a number of international conflicts, including Lebanon, Macedonia, Sudan, and Uganda. Although female participation varies in armies, guerrilla forces, or armed liberation movements, generally they are between one-tenth and one-third of combatants. In Sri Lanka women comprised one-third of the fighting forces (Lindsey 2000; Manoharan 2003); they were one-quarter of the combatants of El Salvador's Farabundo Martí National Liberation Front (FMLN), while in Nicaragua, women were some 30 percent of soldiers and leaders of the Sandinista National Liberation Front (Karame 1999).

Although women and men participate in warfare through a variety of armed bodies, this chapter focuses on their military involvement. It deals with military institutions authorized to use force, such as the army and paramilitaries (referred to as regular armies), and nonstate military actors, such as liberation and guerrilla armies, and traditional militias (referred to as irregular armies). Active participants in conflict are not limited to combat roles, but may also play supporting roles such as cook, porter, administrator, doctor, spy, partner, and sex slave. Moreover, separating soldiers from civilians is often difficult, especially in most intrastate conflicts, where distinctions are blurred due to involvement of irregular armies, the absence of defined battlefields, the use of guerrilla tactics, and combatants that can easily move back and forth between combat and civilian roles.

Male and female civilians may also support the conflict without joining any of the warring parties, for example, by providing moral and logistical support to combatants, broadcasting hate speech, and instilling in the next generation hatred against the enemy or opposing group. Enloe (1998) relates how Serbian feminine ideals (the patriotic mother or the occasional promotion of the woman fighter) were deliberately constructed to bolster the militarization of masculinity. Goldstein (2001) states "the male soldier's construction of his gender identity— masculinity—molds boys from an early age to suppress emotions in order to function more effectively in battle. Women support this system in various ways. The militarized masculinity of men becomes prominent in conflict and is reinforced by women's symbolic embodiment of 'normal life' and by women witnessing male bravery." Enloe (2000) also notes that the militarization of women is necessary for the militarization of men. She asserts that militarization does not always take on the guise of war, but creeps into ordinary daily routines. Militarization is such a pervasive process, and thus so hard to uproot, precisely because it may appear normal or nonthreatening.

Gender Roles in Armies

Men and women may be involved in or actively support conflict for similar reasons including forced recruitment, agreement with the war goals, patriotism, religious or ideological motives, a lack of educational opportunities, and economic necessity (Sörensen 1998). Brett and Specht (2004), however, also point to the different reasons girls and boys give for joining the army. Joining a fighting force is often the only way to survive, but, in some cases, women have joined to obtain equal rights and liberties, as well as to flee or fight oppression. Various

---

Box 2.1 Women Tamil Tigers Take on Combat Roles

In the Tamil movement, women initially performed paramilitary and support roles but were used in combat after 1985. It is currently estimated women comprise 3 out of 10 Central Committee members (highest decision-making body of the Liberation Tigers of Tamil Eelam, LTTE). Of the estimated total cadre strength of 10,000 to 15,000, women account for nearly one-third and are inducted in all of the organization's units—fighting, political, administrative, and intelligence. Reportedly, there is no discrimination based on sex when it comes to training and combat operations, and slogans on "equity for the nation and equality at home" are common. Since women are generally perceived as less dangerous in public places, they have also been used in suicide attacks. However, Manoharan (2003) suggests that it is not clear whether recruitment of women was solely to reinforce social and national freedoms or if it was a response to severe manpower shortages in the mid-1980s.

---

liberation and revolutionary movements have included women's rights and equality for men and women in their programs for political change (Barth 2002; Manoharan 2003) (see box 2.1). In Eritrea, total dedication to the liberation movement erased all other identities of family, region, clan, and class (Barth 2002). In Guinea-Bissau, women were frequently recruited before their husbands because they were totally absorbed by the revolution's ideas (Barth 2002, quoting Urdang 1979). Many Salvadoran women joined the guerrillas hoping it would change their lives and free them from oppression at home and in society at large (Ibañez 2001). Armies often target women for recruitment, particularly to add legitimacy or symbolic power to their war efforts. The female fighter as a symbol was very important in Eritrea and became an important symbol for socialist Yugoslavia. Female soldiers are also recruited because of their desire to prove themselves, which encourages male soldiers to do their best (adapted from Barth 2002). In Mozambique, women and girls were considered more receptive than men and boys to army discipline and new values, and thus more obedient and easier to train.[9] However, the fact that women have been valued by the warring parties should not obscure the fact that many women, like numerous men and boys—as discussed below—join armies against their will, particularly irregular armies.

Women that join armies—voluntarily or forcibly—tend to play three different roles: *combatant, supporter,* and *dependent.* Relatively few women as compared to men operate as combatants who engage

---

Box 2.2 Soldiers in Support Roles Are Excluded
          from Assistance

Female soldiers in support roles—more so than male soldiers—found it
difficult to prove their active participation in war, especially if they were
in irregular armies[10] and consequently were often not included in assistance programs. In Mozambique, women and some men were in support roles and were often not incorporated in the demobilization
program (Baden 1997). In East Timor and Sierra Leone, women without
guns were not involved in demobilization programs (Rehn and Sirleaf
2002; UN 2002). In Sierra Leone's DDR program, ex-combatants initially had to hand in a weapon in exchange for assistance. This one-
person-one-weapon approach was later changed to group disarmament,
in which commanders provided lists of ex-combatants to be disarmed,
but since many women and girls in support roles were not perceived as
soldiers, they were largely excluded from assistance (WCWRC 2002).

---

actively in fighting. Although there are large variations among countries, this is likely because there are many more male than female
soldiers, particularly in regular armies. But underlying notions of masculinity and femininity also tend to associate women less with warfare
than men.

Most women in armies have support and not combat roles. Relatively more women as compared to men operate in armies as cooks,
messengers, health workers, porters, and the like. They are not engaged in fighting and do not carry a weapon. Without a weapon, they
often cannot prove they participated in armies during conflict, which
blocks their access to DDR assistance after conflict [UN Department
for Disarmament Affairs (UNDDA) 2003] (see box 2.2).

Women's third role in armies is that of a dependent. They are the
male combatants' wives, widows, daughters, and other female family
members. They may follow their male counterparts into the bush and
onto the battlefield during conflict. In the same way as their male
counterparts, they need to be reintegrated back into their communities
of origin when the conflict ends.

While in theory these roles can be described separately, in practice
they are hard to distinguish. This is the case, for example, for abducted
women (see box 2.3). In a growing number of conflicts, women have
been abducted into armies, particularly forced to join irregular armies,
subjected to sexual violence and exploitation, and forced to marry
army commanders or officers in their own ranks, which have major
implications for their ability to subsequently reintegrate and become
productive members of society. A key question is whether to regard

---

Box 2.3 Women, Girls, and Boys Are Forcefully
             Recruited into Civil Wars

In Mozambique during the civil war, tens of thousands of girls and boys
were abducted and pressed into service, mainly by the Mozambican National Resistance. Boys younger than eight helped in base camps until
they were old enough for military training; girls were kidnapped for
men's sexual gratification or to cook, clean, and do laundry (de Abreu
1998). A woman in Sierra Leone relates how she was forced to join the
Revolutionary United Front for three years and was made the "wife" of
a man for two years. Many women, especially young girls, were forced
into such marriages, called "jungle marriages," "bush marriages," or
"AK-47 marriages" [Rehn and Sirleaf 2002; Women's Commission for
Refugee Women and Children (WCRWC) 2002]. In Rwanda, women
and girls were detained by military officers and forced to live with them.
Other young girls, mainly Tutsi—called "ceiling girls" because they were
found by the Rwandan Patriotic Front hiding in the ceilings of huts—
were not freed but taken as "war booty." The soldiers who found them
sent them to their superior officers (Turshen and Twagiramariya 1998).
The Tamil Tigers also forcefully conscripted young men and women.

---

these women as dependents of the male combatants who they were
forced to marry or to regard them as women in support functions who
provided sexual services.

The boundaries between the three roles are often blurred because
women combine the roles. They are fighters, spies, cooks, mothers,
and wives at the same time. They fulfill multiple roles that cannot be
separated (adapted from McKay and Mazurana 2004).

Despite these blurred boundaries, most DDR and other post-
conflict rehabilitation programs still provide their assistance on the
basis of artificial splits in women's roles. Mainly, they target female
combatants and hardly—if at all—do they target female supporters
and female dependents. Therefore, the key challenge of post-conflict
rehabilitation programs is to adequately address the needs of all
women who joined armies during conflict, irrespective of whether they
took an active combat role.[11]

Gender Relations in the Army

Traditional relations between women and men change in the military
(Barth 2002; Farr 2002; de Watteville 2002) (see box 2.4). There is a
tendency toward more equal gender relations as compared to those in

Box 2.4 Gender Relations Break with Tradition
in Nepal's Maoist Army

In Nepal, women's involvement in the Maoist army and political cadres
brought about a major break in the social fabric in rural areas. It is reported that every third guerrilla is a woman and that 70 percent of
women guerrillas are from among (the traditionally excluded) indigenous ethnic communities. The girls and women who joined the Maoists
wear combat dress, discarded all jewelry, and cropped their hair short—
they are full of a liberation vocabulary and newfound confidence that
makes ordinary village women question traditional gender roles.
Women and girls who join the Maoists have been systematically sub-
verting the traditional Hindu systems of women's subordination. For
example, they rejected the traditional notion of remaining untouchable
during menstruation and discarded the use of beads and red vermilion
as a marker for married women. Villagers also report that in Maoist-
controlled areas, there has been a decrease in domestic violence,
polygamy, alcohol abuse, and gambling. Of course, it is too early to say
whether these positive changes would develop into sustainable social
norms and values in Nepal's post-conflict rural society, since they are
currently enforced under the threat of violence (CPR 2004).

pre-conflict society. As stated by soldiers: "In armies women ought to
live and act similarly to men" and "women and men become comrades
as soldiers." Men and women in armies tend to share danger, living
conditions, and roles, and often have access to training and education
that is not gender stereotyped.

While women benefit when new opportunities open up, they also
"masculinize," adopting the masculine attitudes and values that prevail
in the army, rather than influencing ("femininizing") the army (Barth
2002). Although women clearly benefit from more egalitarian gender
relations in armies, this is generally more than offset by the frequency
of sexual slavery and violence against women and girls by armies.
Mackay and Mazurama (2004) found that egalitarian gender relationships in fighting forces were not evident in the three post-conflict countries they studied—instead they concluded that women and girls were
subjected to oppression, gender-specific violence, and abusive and
violent relationships, with rare opportunities to exercise autonomy.

In the case where relatively more egalitarian gender relations are
prevalent in armed forces, these tend to revert to pre-existing patterns
when peace arrives. Whereas all ex-combatants from both regular and
irregular armies have difficulties reintegrating into civilian life, the

process is often more complex for female soldiers, especially because reintegration tends to go hand-in-hand with the reintroduction of pre-conflict gender relations (e.g., Baden 1997). Female soldiers need to reassimilate into a society where gender stereotypes are much more rigidly upheld than within the military (Farr 2002, quoting Shikola 1998). Moreover, as discussed later in this report, female ex-combatants face a number of additional issues such as health, raising children from rape, ostracism, and domestic violence. Female ex-combatants often opt not to return to their communities, but instead remain in exile or relocate to avoid reverting to traditional ways of living and restrictive social norms.

Development Challenges: Providing Post-Conflict Assistance to Female Ex-Soldiers

The key challenges for DDR and other post-conflict rehabilitation programs are to identify and target all women who joined the (ir)regular armies and to provide them with adequate assistance.

Until now, most assistance to women in armies tended to be provided through DDR programs, which generally begin operating on the heels of a peace accord or when the security situation permits. However, for a number of reasons the DDR assistance does not reach women in armies. First, some DDR programs tend not to target women in armies at all. This relates to the fact that the overriding rationale behind DDR programs is to increase security by disarming combatants and that social objectives are of secondary consideration. DDR programs are not primarily meant to reward or assist combatants, but are designed to restore security by "keeping them off the street" (Specht 2003) or "buying the peace" (Arthy 2003). As female combatants are not directly regarded as a major security threat, they are not generally targeted by DDR programs, as was the case in Mozambique, Sierra Leone, and a number of other countries.

Second, as DDR program resources are invariably scarce, they tend to be narrowly targeted and adopt a narrow definition of an ex-combatant. They usually only target female ex-combatants with a weapon. But even if women carry a weapon, they may still find it difficult to prove that they were active combatants, especially if there is group disarmament (see box 2.2); women have to rely on male superiors for confirmation of their combatant status and hence eligibility for DDR support (de Watteville 2002).

Third, even if DDR programs are willing to offer support to all women that joined (ir)regular armies, they cannot easily track them, as these women tend to disappear quickly from the scene when the fighting ends. There are several reasons for this occurrence. One is that women's participation in conflict may become "invisible" or minimized in the post-conflict phase, because traditional gender relations are reintroduced and women are expected to revert to more traditional and less visible roles. This tendency is well expressed in the French saying: *Il y a plus inconnu que le soldat, c'est sa femme* (there is one more unknown than the soldier, it's his wife) (Karame 1999). As Shikola (1998) notes in the case of Namibia: "Men appreciate women who cook for them and they respect women who fought in the war with them, but after independence they did not really consider women as part of the liberation struggle." This appears to be true in other countries such as El Salvador, Eritrea, Ethiopia, and Guatemala. Another reason is that women do not want to reveal their identity as female combatants, out of fear of stigmatization and association with killings, sexual violence, rape, illegitimate children, and sexual promiscuity (see box 2.5).

Yet another reason is that women—particularly abducted women who forcibly became the "wives" of soldiers and who in some situations are considered the "rewards" of their captors—do not wait for a DDR program to start, but escape from the army as soon as possible (see box 2.6). In the McKay and Mazurana (2004) study of Mozambique, Sierra Leone, and Uganda, they refer to this process as spontaneous reintegration—a large number of girls spontaneously found their way home and thus did not receive DDR benefits or social reintegration assistance to provide physical, material, or psychosocial help. They often face huge demobilization and reintegration challenges and frequently end up in isolation and extreme poverty after the conflict ends.

Box 2.5 Female Soldiers Hide Their Identity

"Targeting female soldiers is a problem when women do not want to be recognized as combatants after a war is over because of stigma attached to this. An example comes from Liberia, where many women wanted to hide the fact that they had been soldiers. Such women are hard to find— 'You can't find them, it is like they never existed' (Bennett 1995)—and consequently they never received any benefits after the war. . . . Not only in the case of Liberia, but other cases as well, ex-combatant women are well known to face difficulties in getting accepted in traditional society, and the consequence may be that they do not come forward to receive the assistance they are entitled to, but on the contrary hide their identity." (Barth 2002)

Box 2.6 Abducted Women in Sierra Leone Flee from the Army

Although the Sierra Leone DDR program is regarded as a success, it did not pay sufficient attention to the needs of women and girls who played a support role in the army or those that were forced to act as the "wives" and "sex slaves" of army commanders. After the conflict, many of these women and girls took the opportunity to get away from their "husbands" without receiving demobilization and reintegration assistance. Even those who stayed did not receive assistance, as they were considered the dependents of demobilizing male soldiers and not granted individual rights. Hardly any protection and support was available if they opted out or managed to escape these relations. A few efforts were made to provide them with protection and reintegration support, but these were largely outside the official DDR program (WCRWC 2002).

To improve post-conflict assistance that is provided to women that joined (ir)regular armies, DDR programs should not only be gender-sensitized, but they should also be complemented by parallel rehabilitation programs that incorporate a gender dimension. *The main challenge is to arrive at an appropriate division of labor between DD(R) and additional rehabilitation programs that fully takes into account the different and often complex roles played by women (and men) in the fighting forces and the implications for their reintegration.* The key is to ensure that reintegration activities are gender sensitized—engendering the "R" in DDR.

Arthy makes a suggestion for such a division of labor. Based on his evaluation of the Sierra Leone experience, Arthy (2003) argues that, in future DDR efforts, one organization should conduct combatant disarmament and demobilization, and an entirely separate organization should be responsible for the reintegration of both ex-combatants and noncombatants. He argues that this division could also stimulate a much more direct linkage between more general community recovery projects and the reintegration challenge. This delinking would presumably make it easier to adopt a more comprehensive and engendered approach to reintegration activities.[12] Reintegration activities could be much better adapted to the different needs and skills of male and female ex-combatants in areas such as security, (reproductive) health, education, employment, and information dissemination (Farr 2002). It may ensure that reintegration processes do not contribute to the restoration of pre-conflict gender roles, but instead try to capitalize on positive gender roles during conflict. And it may contribute to more transformative reintegration programs, including information and sensitization campaigns on equal rights for women and men, and on their roles and responsibilities in society. Community-based reintegration programs for both ex-combatants and noncombatants avoid the perception that violence is being rewarded, lessen distrust, and improve prospects for social reconciliation between different conflict-affected groups. They also make it easier for ex-combatants to access reintegration assistance as they are not obliged to reveal their past as combatants. Ex-combatants benefit from being in a larger group that includes women in the communities, if the focus is on longer-term capacity building. For example, reintegration programs may strengthen local service providers' capacity to deliver effective assistance to returning ex-combatants and noncombatants (adapted from Specht 2003).

Still to be worked out in practice and in each context are the modalities of the division of labor between (security) agencies dealing with disarmament and demobilization activities and (rehabilitation) agencies focusing on reintegration activities. Although the labor division is largely based on an artificial split in women's roles—those with a weapon versus those without a weapon—it may well improve the assistance provided to *all* women that participated in the armies. Ideally, security agencies target women with weapons—and often unarmed female family members of male combatants with weapons—with disarmament and demobilization assistance, and after that rehabilitation and reintegration agencies provide reintegration assistance. As for women without weapons—women in support roles and/or abducted women who want to receive assistance separate from their male counterparts—they will generally only receive reintegration assistance that the rehabilitation agencies provide.

However, effective assistance to these two groups of women in armies requires careful coordination and fine-tuning between and among the security and rehabilitation agencies involved. For example, the agencies would need to:

- Jointly or in a coordinated manner *track and identify* women in armies well before the start of their programs, so as to prevent women's self-demobilization as much as possible;
- Ensure that women can *smoothly transition from the demobilization to the reintegration phase* and do not drop out;
- Find ways to *balance the assistance* provided to women with weapons and women without weapons. The amount of assistance provided during disarmament and demobilization should be relatively low as compared to that given during reintegration. This will avoid "overassisting" women with weapons and

"underassisting" those without weapons. It could also lessen tensions and rivalries between the two groups.

• Discuss how women that only receive reintegration assistance would be prepared for their return home and their transport home. Agencies may need to first bring the women together at reception/rehabilitation centers before they return home and start receiving the actual reintegration assistance.

• Consider the extent to which rehabilitation agencies want to *link specific reintegration programs for women who joined the army with broader community-recovery programs* that *target all returning and recipient community members*. Women that joined the army constitute a separate group with special needs, but it could be more appropriate not to target them separately so that they do not have to hide their identity as combatants.

• Find ways that rehabilitation agencies could ensure *women's protection*—particularly abducted women—against renewed violence by their male counterparts. They should avoid at all costs the possibility that abducted women are reintegrated into the same communities as the "husbands" they attempted to flee from.

• Jointly consider *funding issues*. Ideally, funding should be balanced between disarmament and demobilization activities for women with weapons and reintegration activities for all women who joined the army. This would avoid a continuation of the current situation whereby those with weapons receive assistance and those without weapons do not. One suggestion is to establish one fund for disarmament and demobilization activities, and reintegration activities. The establishment of one fund or at least the strong coordination in mobilizing funding would help to ensure closer coordination of disarmament and demobilization activities with implementation of reintegration activities, irrespective of overall funding availability for both activities.

• Agree on the *timing* of the reintegration activities in particular. Arthy (2003) points out that while armed groups remained in Sierra Leone, efforts focused almost entirely on disarming and demobilizing the groups, but reintegration activities were generally not well integrated with disarmament and demobilization activities. Coupled with the interrupted and then phased nature of disarmament and demobilization, this meant that many ex-combatants had to wait more than a year to gain access to a reintegration program. As most women will probably only receive reintegration assistance, this puts women at a considerable disadvantage if they have to wait for ex-combatant women and men to first go through the disarmament and demobilization phase. Instead, to the extent possible, reintegration activities for these women have to be prepared well in advance and should be implemented *in parallel with* the disarmament and demobilization activities. If such a parallel implementation of reintegration activities cannot be ensured, the notion of a division of labor between security and rehabilitation agencies would need to be reconsidered, as there would be a high risk that women without weapons will not wait for reintegration assistance and instead opt for self-demobilization. In that case, women—and those without weapons—should be given access to benefits under the entire DDR program; this would better ensure their access to assistance than the option described above.

Policy Options

The recommended policy options build on the suggested division of labor between security agencies and rehabilitation and reintegration agencies. Policy options indicate whether they apply to security agencies that provide disarmament and demobilization assistance, to the rehabilitation agencies that handle reintegration, or to both. As pointed out by Arthy (2003), the reintegration component of a DDR program must be an integral part of a post-conflict recovery strategy to avoid the risk that the whole reintegration effort will be viewed as merely re-establishing the old failed order. For both DDR programs and post-conflict reconstruction more broadly, a post-conflict needs assessment is a good place to start. The recently completed *Practical Guide on Needs Assessments* that the Deutsche Gesellschaft für Technische Zusammenarbeit (GTZ) prepared for the World Bank and UNDP/UN Development Group (UNDG) presents a useful and comprehensive gender checklist to be addressed as a crosscutting theme in the needs assessment (Kievelitz et al. 2004). The guide (see the bibliography) notes that gender mainstreaming needs to start from the very beginning of a needs assessment mission to ensure that structures and programs are designed to address the different requirements of women and men, including their needs for protection, assistance, justice, and reconstruction.

Provide Post-Conflict Assistance to All Women and Men in (Ir)regular Armies

- *Recast the definition of female combatant.* To avoid gender discrimination, the beneficiaries of post-conflict assistance must be clearly defined. In particular, more generic guidelines and criteria for the definition of a female ex-combatant are needed so as to avoid the situation where women associated with the armed groups become ineligible for assistance or that abducted women are regarded only as dependents of male fighters and not as combatants that are granted rights and benefits. For example, programs must not focus exclusively on women with weapons, as this excludes many women in armies without a weapon, nor should they be skewed toward the higher ranks that are usually occupied by men; they should also pay attention to the lower ranks where most women are employed. Furthermore, agencies should treat carefully the lists that warlords and commanders provide that define who was under their command; women tend not to figure on these lists and priority is given to favored males. All in all, security and rehabilitation agencies should consider redefining female combatants as: *women who are part of an (ir)regular army in any capacity including, but not limited to, cooks, porters, messengers, and the like, and including women recruited for forced sexual purposes and/or forced marriage* to jointly ensure that all female combatants are targeted with adequate assistance.

- *Track and identify female and male ex-combatants well in advance of the DDR program.* Irrespective of whether ex-combatants will only receive reintegration assistance, or disarmament and demobilization assistance as well, the agencies must track and identify them from the start. As indicated above, various female combatants tend to self-demobilize and disappear long before the start of any post-conflict assistance program. To avoid this, security and rehabilitation agencies need to make extra efforts to track female ex-combatants when the planning phase starts. For instance, they may hire gender experts to conduct needs assessment missions among women that are still in the army. In these missions, gender experts may discuss what women in armies expect from assistance programs, how their reluctance to join these programs can be overcome, how these programs can best ensure their protection against (sexual) violence, and how to best avoid stigmatization as a female combatant. Without explicit efforts to track and identify female combatants in the planning phase, they will remain underreported. Once, but only if, female combatants sign up for assistance, the security and rehabilitation agencies can decide who is to receive what form of assistance.

- *Consider targeting female dependents of male ex-combatants in their own right and separately from their male counterparts.* In various DDR programs dependents are regarded as secondary instead of primary beneficiaries. Benefits are often calculated based on the family and given to the soldier, but since the soldier may misuse the benefits, there is a need to monitor whether assistance reaches the intended targets (de Watteville 2002). Arthy (2003) notes that in Sierra Leone there was a worrying tendency for male ex-combatants to forcibly, and often violently, take loans away from their wives; their wives had benefited from a microcredit program that supported small enterprise development and was targeted to women. The establishment of selection and monitoring committees where strong and dedicated women (and men) are represented has proven useful in adopting more gender-sensitive selection criteria (de Watteville 2002; Barth 2002). In Eritrea's demobilization and reintegration program (1993–97), where 13,500 out of 54,000 demobilized fighters were women, National Union of Eritrean Women representatives participated in a special committee that studied demobilization and reintegration procedures and surveyed fighters that were to be demobilized (Bruchhaus and Mehreteab 2000). Although steps can be taken to make selection and eligibility criteria more gender sensitive, there has been little work undertaken to evaluate actual use of and access to the services provided.

Besides improving how women receive assistance as secondary beneficiaries, security and rehabilitation agencies may well consider targeting women—particularly abducted women and widows—in their own right and separately from their male counterparts. Instead of targeting them as dependents of male ex-combatants in a DDR program, they can be provided with reintegration assistance separately from their male counterparts. To implement this policy option, security and rehabilitation agencies should assess whether and how women want to receive assistance separately from their male counterparts throughout the planning phase.

• *Improve access to information on DDR programs.* Disseminating information can help ensure a more balanced selection of female and male combatants, but it is often difficult to reach all ex-combatants with information on DDR benefits, eligibility, and assistance. More effective information dissemination can help encourage female and male combatants to sign up for assistance, recognizing that women frequently have less access to information than men. In addition to television and radio, the use of women-targeted communication channels (such as health centers, churches, and schools) should be considered (de Watteville 2002; Barth 2002). Information on how they will be protected and separated from their male colleagues in the disarmament and demobilization process and on the provision of facilities such as childcare may also increase the number of women who will apply for disarmament, demobilization, and/or reintegration assistance.

Gender-Sensitizing Demobilization Efforts

The following suggestions are especially relevant for security agencies that aim to disarm and demobilize male and female combatants with weapons. They are also relevant for rehabilitation agencies, however, since they also have a role to play as part of the reintegration process in preparing female combatants for their return home.

- *Use the momentum that demobilization generates to prepare women and men to return to civilian life.* Demobilization represents a unique opportunity to make female and male ex-combatants aware of their rights as civilians in the post-conflict phase. It is also the moment to introduce ex-combatants to support structures and civil society organizations. These organizations can help them to exercise their rights and continue to organize after conflict. Remaining organized can provide ex-combatants with critical support in reintegration because the camaraderie that soldiers derived from fighting usually vanishes during demobilization when they are dispersed (Meintjes et al. 2001). For women, being organized may also increase the chance of upholding the more equal gender relations enjoyed in some armies. Thus, integration of ex-combatants into existing or new frameworks, such as veteran groups and women's organizations, should be considered in the demobilization phase. At the same time, however, there is a need to anticipate certain risks. When ex-combatants remain organized on the basis of their wartime roles, this may constrain the reintegration process or exacerbate the risk of future instability. Finally, the demobilization phase is also an excellent moment to ensure that government authorities are aware that female soldiers exist and need to be included in the planning and funding of reintegration programs (Farr 2002).
- *Consider adjusting demobilization activities and facilities.* Demobilization needs to be tailored to the specific needs of ex-soldiers in terms of their socioeconomic and educational background (Oklahoma 1999). Ideally, all steps in the process need to

be gender-sensitized. The steps include: assembly in encampments, pre-discharge information, registration and distribution of identity cards, medical screening with a special emphasis on HIV/AIDS, and transport home. Encampments must guarantee women's safety, for example, through guards or fenced quarters and install special facilities suitable for women, men, and children, such as separate sanitation facilities, food adapted to children's needs, and distribution of appropriate clothing. If such security measures are not taken, then the risk of higher dropout rates increases substantially. Pre-discharge information must correspond to women's and men's needs; it may cover topics such as land and inheritance rights, access to credit, access to education and employment, difficult social acceptance in the community of settlement, and domestic violence. Involving a gender specialist in these programs should be required. Finally, there must be appropriate health provisions, including reproductive and children's health facilities and appropriate numbers of female and male staff.[13] Providing this information during encampment is preferable, but ex-combatants can also be targeted at their arrival point and at the host communities (e.g., Colletta et al. 1996a).

Gender-Sensitizing the Reintegration of Female and Male Ex-Combatants

In general, rehabilitation agencies are responsible for reintegrating combatants. On the one hand, they have to deal with the women that first entered the demobilization and reintegration trajectory, and on the other hand, with the women that directly enter the reintegration trajectory. Particularly the latter still need to be prepared for reintegration and carefully protected against their so-called "husbands" and other male counterparts they tried to escape from. At the same time, rehabilitation agencies have to consider how to target the needs of female and male ex-combatants, but also of their families and host communities (e.g., UNDDA 2003), and how to link their reintegration programs to broader community-recovery programs.

The following policy options could render economic, social, and psychological reintegration efforts more gender-sensitive:[14]

- *Adapt reintegration activities to the different needs and possibilities of female and male ex-combatants.* Economic reintegration for all combatants is generally complicated due to the scarcity of land, lack of employment opportunities, and low skill and education levels. The process is usually more difficult for female soldiers as they are expected to revert to pre-conflict labor patterns, face legal restrictions on land ownership and inheritance, and have limited mobility, especially if they are responsible for children and other dependents.

Whereas the economic reintegration of ex-combatants in rural areas is usually difficult due to the lack of access to land, credit, and labor, their reintegration in urban settings is often no less complicated. Although women and men may well find a job in the urban informal sector, it is often much harder to obtain employment in the urban formal sector simply because there are hardly any formal jobs available in the war-torn economies, and competition on the labor market is high. On the one hand, reintegration programs for ex-combatants may increase their chances for formal employment, while on the other hand various cases (Ethiopia and Namibia) show that low skills and education make ex-combatants ill-equipped to find formal employment (e.g., Colletta et al. 1996; Kingma 1996). In Mozambique, many women [International Labor Organization (ILO) 1997; Barth 2002 quoting Arthur 1998] entered the army at such an early age that they had little education or work experience (Baden 1997). Female ex-combatants also tend to face more difficulties entering formal labor markets, because of a return to pre-conflict labor patterns and because they are often associated only with informal work.

In addition to ensuring that former male and female combatants receive adequate economic assistance, DDR programs should also consider how to increase the economic absorptive capacity of host communities and local economies, which has proven a difficult challenge in most post-conflict countries. Ideally, local economic revival initiatives, such as community-driven development projects, should be part and parcel of DDR programs. In addition, they should be based on careful gender analysis, highlighting the potentials and constraints of women, especially female-headed households, and men to access employment and generate incomes. Such projects not only improve the effectiveness of DDR programs, but also benefit male and female beneficiaries living in the host communities.

• *Facilitate equally the social reintegration of female and male ex-combatants.* Whereas emphasis is usually placed on the economic independence of ex-combatants, it is often their difficulty in reintegrating into social networks that proves to be the most challenging (Kingma 1996). This may be especially difficult for female combatants because they have to take on their earlier family roles, which are strikingly different from their roles and positions during warfare (e.g., Colletta et al. 1996; Oklahoma 1999). They are often accused of promiscuity during conflict and face exclusion and ostracism. In addition, as pointed out by McKay and Mazurana (2004) in the three countries studied, girls that spent time in fighting forces were reported to display difficult behavior—such as being aggressive, quarrelsome, and using abusive language—violating gender norms and affecting their ability to readjust to their community and the community's response to them. In the case of Sierra Leone, they point out that it was easier for communities to accept troublesome boys because "boys will be boys" but troublesome girls were much harder to reintegrate. Thus, social reintegration must not only facilitate the transition of combatants and their dependents into civilian life, but also help to reshape societal and community attitudes toward them (Farr 2002).

Often, communities do not willingly accept returning ex-combatants, regarding them as conveyors of diseases such as HIV/AIDS, violence, and misbehavior. One option is to prepare the community for the return of ex-combatants through information campaigns or by training community leaders. Another option is to establish community development projects, such as mediation, conflict resolution, education, local infrastructure rehabilitation programs, or income-generating activities, which bring the community and ex-combatants together and often improve the social reintegration of ex-soldiers. In both cases, it is especially important to prepare the community for the return of soldiers' wives and female ex-soldiers. Their social reintegration is often more complicated and requires extra attention. Soldiers' wives, especially if they have a different background than their husbands, are frequently isolated by their husband's community and even by their husbands, often with little or no financial and social support. Many female ex-combatants face problems because the community may not accept their involvement in the army, whether it was voluntary or forced, and because they are associated with sexual violence and promiscuity. Consequently, a substantial number of female ex-soldiers divorce or become unmarriageable, frustrating their social and economic reintegration [e.g., Colletta et al. 1996; Kingma 1997; Bonn International Center for Conversion (BICC) 2002].

An option may be to encourage purification rites, which can help the community to accept these women and the women to deal with their trauma (de Watteville 2002). Although there is evidence that such rites have facilitated the social reintegration of ex-combatants, particularly child soldiers,[15] we do not know how prevalent they are or what their impact is on female ex-soldiers and soldiers' wives. McKay and Mazurana (2004) found that rituals in Mozambique, Sierra Leone, and Uganda were used to assist some girls in healing and reintegrating into their communities. Among the community-based rituals were those that welcome the child back and cleansing rituals that drive out dead spirits, protect the community from contamination by evil influences, and call on ancestors for assistance. The cleansing washes off the blood of war, which can contaminate the community. Some rituals are gender specific—in Mozambique and Sierra Leone rituals have helped sexually abused girls; in Mozambique older women are in charge of healing rituals. A Northern Ugandan girl was made to step on an egg, to symbolize taking on a new life. In Mozambique, once a person undergoes a traditional ritual, they are not allowed to speak of the trauma again. However, special sensitivity is required since not all rituals are safe or appropriate. Some rituals violate women's human rights, are often patriarchal in nature, and can be detrimental to women's health and well-being. An example is when initiation rituals involve genital mutilation performed by female members of secret societies for a girl to be accepted back into society (McKay and Mazurana 2004). Local women's NGOs can take the lead in assessing initiation and reintegration rituals, as well as counseling and supporting reintegration of female ex-soldiers and soldiers' wives (Oklahoma 1999).

Besides encouraging ex-combatants to integrate into existing social networks, another option is to establish and promote networks among ex-soldiers, such as veterans' groups. Networks may provide a safe place to exchange views, to discuss working opportunities, to become organized, and to build confidence. Agencies should consider supporting separate networks for female and male ex-soldiers, because of the sensitivity of the issues involved and because of their possible different needs and interests (see box 2.7). Whether to form mixed groups of civilians and ex-combatants is still debated. Some argue that the mixed-group approach often has not worked, because of the different positions in the community (Colletta et al. 1996), while others state that mixed groups will help ex-combatants in changing their military identity into a civilian one (e.g., Specht 2003).

Finally, agencies may target the relatively large number of female ex-soldiers who feel that reintegrating at home is impossible because the changes they have undergone are too great to readjust to

---

Box 2.7 Mozambique's AMODEG, a Veterans'
Organization, Reaches Out to Women

In 1994, the veterans' organization AMODEG formed a women's branch in response to the fact that only men's issues were being addressed and began to lobby for equal rights for female ex-soldiers. It focused on issues such as women's entitlement to resettlement allowances, proper clothing for women, psychological support for both women and men, specific economic reintegration courses for women, and the idea that former soldiers should be considered as a heterogeneous group including men, women, children, and disabled combatants (Date-Bah and Walsh 2001).

---

conventional life. These women opt to go elsewhere, often placing themselves outside family and community support networks (e.g., BICC 2002) and limiting their access to assistance under existing programs (Barth 2002). This reinforces the need to widely disseminate information on reintegration using different channels such as churches, mosques, and health centers. Particularly for one of the less visible groups of ex-combatants, namely, girls and women who voluntarily choose not to sign up for reintegration assistance, agencies should find ways to target and include them in their programs.

- *Rely on and support existing informal community efforts that are often led by women to support social reintegration.* As described in box 2.8, below, local community initiatives to assist in reintegration often emerge spontaneously. These are often ignored by development actors and should be supported. Supporting the work of these women can be an effective and essential ingredient to ensure sustainable reintegration.
- *Provide psychological counseling to female and male ex-combatants.*[16] Conflict and the transition to peace are mentally demanding for ex-combatants, and many need psychological assistance. They may show typical signs of trauma, such as depression, psychological disabilities, chronic fatigue, and recurrent recollections of traumatic incidents. The need for culturally appropriate counseling in DDR programs is increasingly accepted, especially if ex-soldiers cannot be referred to other psychological counseling services. However, the mental recovery of ex-soldiers is a long-term and time-consuming process that normally exceeds the period of DDR programs. Besides ensuring that follow-up assistance is available, agencies must try to ensure that mental

---

Box 2.8 Women Support Reintegration in Sierra Leone

Across Sierra Leone as individuals and in groups, women have been critical to the reintegration of former combatants, particularly those excluded from official programs. In a study by Women Waging Peace
(2004), 55 percent of the respondents indicated that women in the community played a significant role in helping them reintegrate. This was
higher than responses for the assistance they received from traditional
leaders (20 percent) or international aid workers (32 percent). They said
community women provided guidance, shared meager resources, and
helped facilitate their skills training and education by providing childcare, clothes, and food. Moreover, women's organizations also represented models for many of the female ex-combatants—more than 65 percent of respondents stated they would like to join such organizations,
which they saw as offering practical assistance. Local community efforts,
informal networks, and organizations—primarily led by women—can
provide critical support for former combatants. Unlike the international
community, they have no exit strategy—if they fail, violence returns to
their doorstep. They have scarce resources, their work is rarely acknowledged in official processes, and they receive only limited assistance from
the international community (Mazurana and Carlson 2004).

---

health programs are accessible to women and men, for example
through women-to-women and men-to-men counseling, and
that they are sensitized to their particular needs. Whereas the
psychological needs of female and male ex-combatants may not
necessarily differ, specific problems may arise for female ex-
soldiers because society does not always show sympathy for
their refusal to return to traditional roles and submissive behavior, as is often expected of them (e.g., Bruchhaus and Mehreteab
2000). Moreover, it is likely that more women than men suffer
psychologically from gender-based and sexual violence committed against them in conflict.

CHAPTER 3

Gender-Based and Sexual Violence: A Multidimensional Approach

Overview

IN THIS BOOK, GBV is defined as physical, sexual, and psychological violence against both men and women that occurs within the family and the community and is perpetrated or condoned by the state. In conflict situations, GBV is committed against civilians and soldiers. It is not an accidental side effect of war, but a crime against the individual and an act of aggression against the entire community or nation.

Regarding *gender-specific roles* related to GBV, women are more vulnerable to GBV than men because of prevailing oppressive gender relations. This also applies to conflict situations. More women than men lack mobility and are unarmed and unprotected at a time when traditional forms of moral, community, and institutional safeguards disintegrate and weapons proliferate, which makes them particularly vulnerable to all kinds of violations, such as rape as an organized form of warfare. The trafficking in and sexual exploitation of human beings, particularly of women, tends to increase in conflict situations. Many women engage in prostitution to survive conflict, but also because sex becomes a form of bargaining power. Widespread GBV during conflict increases the spread of sexually transmitted diseases (STDs) such as HIV/AIDS, especially among women.

One of the *changes* in GBV relates to its intensity. GBV is frequently rooted in pre-conflict conditions, but it increases and often becomes an accepted practice during conflict and in the post-conflict phase. In addition, with the transition from conflict to peace, a shift in GBV seems to take place from the public to the private domain through an increase in domestic violence.

A major *development challenge* is to support the protection and recovery of GBV survivors. This could best be done via a multidimensional approach that actively involves GBV survivors, their communities, the health sector, social services, and the legal and security sectors. This approach needs to involve men explicitly, not only as bystanders and perpetrators in need of alternative notions of nonmilitarized masculinity, but also as GBV survivors who are in need of assistance.

GBV *policies* need to target both men and women. Awareness needs to be raised to ensure that GBV in conflict is acknowledged and addressed in post-conflict reconstruction and that local capacity to provide psychological counseling is strengthened to reach all actors involved (survivors, survivors' families, witnesses, and perpetrators). In this situation, using or integrating local traditional counseling techniques or community-based counseling approaches with western techniques should be considered. However, these should not be used without assessing their potentially different impacts on female and male GBV survivors. Agencies should also strengthen the medical assistance provided to GBV survivors; this would encompass improving the performance of those who provide medical support directly to GBV survivors, such as doctors and other health workers, but also of those who are indirectly involved, such as social workers, community health workers, traditional practitioners, and Ministry of Health staff. Women and men should have similar protection against GBV, have the same information on and access to GBV medical services, and be assisted by a same-sex health worker (and translator) during medical examinations. Agencies should further encourage the legal protection of women and men against GBV through existing laws and newly adopted legislation. In addition, the police, judiciary, border guards, and the social services system need institutional capacity building to better assist GBV survivors.

GBV and Conflict

GBV includes: (i) physical, sexual, and psychological violence occurring in the family, such as the sexual abuse of girls, dowry-related violence, marital rape, female genital mutilation and other traditional practices harmful to women, nonspousal violence, and violence-related exploitation; (ii) physical, sexual, and psychological violence occurring in the community, including rape, sexual abuse, sexual harassment and intimidation at work, in educational institutions, and elsewhere, trafficking in women, and forced prostitution; and (iii) physical, sexual, and psychological violence perpetrated or condoned by the state, wherever it occurs. Both men and women experience GBV.

As intrastate conflicts have increased, civilians have become the main victims. In recent decades, the proportion of war victims who are civilians has leaped dramatically to an estimated 75 percent [UN Secretary-General (UNSG) 2001] or higher, most of them probably women and children.[17] Regarding GBV, "we know that 94% of displaced households in Sierra Leone have experienced sexual assaults including rape, torture, and sexual slavery, and that at least 250,000—perhaps as many as 500,000—women were raped during the 1994 genocide in Rwanda" (Rehn and Sirleaf 2002). GBV does not occur "accidentally" or as a side effect of warfare as is sometimes suggested. Rather, it is consciously planned and targeted. GBV is strategic violence that is aimed at intimidating and demoralizing the enemy. GBV is both a crime against the individual and an act of aggression against the entire community or nation. Women—as symbolic bearers of caste, ethnic, or national identity—are systematically violated. From a cultural perspective, the entire community is affected. As Nordstrom (1991) states: "Rape, as with all terror warfare, is not exclusively an attack on the body—it is an attack on the 'body politic.' Its goal is not to maim or kill one person, but to control an entire sociopolitical process by crippling it. It is an attack directed equally against personal identity and cultural integrity." In intrastate wars, most nonstate protagonists do not feel bound by internationally agreed conventions or to the same degree as states. This does not preclude widespread violations by state actors as well.

Gender-Specific Roles: Types of GBV

As a consequence of unequal gender relations, women are generally more vulnerable to violence than men. This also applies to conflict situations where more women than men remain unarmed and unprotected. Concurrently, traditional forms of moral, community, and institutional safeguards have disintegrated and weapons have proliferated, making women particularly vulnerable to all kinds of violations [International Committee of the Red Cross (ICRC) 2001]. Because women normally have to bear greater responsibility than men for their children and elderly relatives, they are less able to flee and escape violence. Forced displacement may also subject more women than men to violations of their physical integrity and safety. A lack of gender sensitivity in refugee camps may also expose women to risk and violence; for example, the camps may not have well-protected women's quarters or may have inappropriate sanitary facilities.

GBV tends to increase in conflict situations. GBV has become a means of warfare; it can be a result of a general breakdown in law and order and a policy to demoralize the enemy (Byrne 1996). Moreover, sex can come to be seen as a form of reward or war booty that unpaid, underfed, and drugged or intoxicated fighters demand. GBV's effects on survivors can range from psychological problems and traumas to social exclusion and even ostracism of those involved and the children born from sexual violence (e.g., Human Rights Watch 1996). Because of the disruption of social order and traditional institutions in wartime, GBV—which would normally provoke strong community reactions and sanctions—frequently goes unpunished in conflict. While GBV affects men, male GBV survivors have been overlooked. Men and boys are raped during conflict, and men become targets of sexual abuse, torture, and mutilation to attack and destroy their sense of masculinity or manhood (UN 2002). There are indications that during conflict, men who resist taking part in the war or object to it and homosexuals face more problems.

Trafficking in and sexual exploitation of human beings tend to increase during conflict. The breakdown of law and order, police functions, and border controls, combined with globalization's fluid markets and open borders, contributes to an increase in the trafficking of human beings. The connection between conflict and trafficking becomes even more apparent as criminal networks involved in the arms and drug trade expand to include trafficking in human beings. Although it is difficult to document, the majority of trafficked persons are women (Rehn and Sirleaf 2002). Corrin (2004) points out that different approaches to handling trafficking have different gender impacts.[18]

Women often resort to prostitution as a coping mechanism to survive conflict, as it offers a source of income and a form of bargaining power. More women than men are forced into commercial sex in a desperate attempt to survive. They may become sexually involved with members of armed groups or with people that provide food, shelter, safe passage, and other needs in exchange for sex, as well as with relatively well-off international agency personnel (e.g., El-Bushra 2003; Rehn and Sirleaf 2002).

Closely related to GBV is the spread of STDs, including HIV/AIDS. Although many countries with high STD infection rates have not been at war, there is evidence that conflict contributes to HIV/AIDS transmission. Complex social factors play a role, such as the displacement that separates families, the disintegration of communities and family life, and the breakup of stable relationships. Other factors include the disruption of social norms governing sexual behavior and fatalism among soldiers and civilians in war situations. The military are particularly at risk—STD infection rates among armed forces are generally two to five times higher than among civilians, although during conflict the difference can be over 50 times (Rehn and Sirleaf 2002). This is largely because troops are usually young, sexually active, male, single, and, in some armies, actively discouraged from marrying (Carballo et al. 2000).

Survival sex, GBV as a war strategy, and unsanitary medical procedures also contribute to increasing HIV/AIDS transmission in conflict situations. The lethal nexus between HIV/AIDS and conflict is particularly serious for women. A complex interaction between biological factors and socially constructed gender roles places women at greater risk of contracting HIV/AIDS during conflict. Their experience is gender specific in three important respects that involve rape, women's vulnerability, and the HIV/AIDS stigma (adapted from Saferworld/International Alert 2004).

1. Women are particularly at risk through rape. In addition to the psychological and physical violence, the possibility of HIV infection through rape causes further anxiety among the victims, which is worsened by the stigma that often accompanies women who have been raped.
2. Women are more vulnerable as they form the majority of refugees and internally displaced persons (IDPs). In many refugee camps, women have little choice but to trade sex in return for vital needs, thereby increasing their infection risk. In times of conflict, family members or spouses may sell women into sexual slavery.
3. Women can be stigmatized for bearing HIV-positive children, who may have been fathered by "the enemy," and sometimes because they are mistakenly identified as being responsible for AIDS. It is often women and girls who are left to care for children orphaned by AIDS. Hence, HIV/AIDS and STD issues need to be addressed in armies and in DDR programs,[19] with an expanded focus on female ex-combatants, soldiers' wives, and women in the receiving communities.

Dynamics: A GBV Continuum

Civilians in conflict face a GBV continuum, which is frequently rooted in pre-conflict conditions, exacerbated during conflict, and continues in the post-conflict phase. GBV does not arise solely from wartime conditions but is also directly related to the violence that exists in women's and men's lives during peacetime (Rehn and Sirleaf 2002). GBV becomes an accepted practice that can continue after hostilities have ceased. Sideris (2000) notes that war has left men with "either an eroded sense of manhood or the option of a militarized masculine identity with the attendant legitimization of violence and killing as a way of maintaining a sense of power and control. . . . Questions of how to provide men with alternative notions of masculinity and a positive role in reconstruction are crucial in transition periods if we are effectively to address discourses that legitimate violence against women."

A shift in GBV seems to take place from the public to the private domain in the transition from conflict to peace. Obviously, domestic violence is common during peacetime, but it tends to increase in post-conflict situations because of the continued availability of weapons, the violence that male family members have experienced or meted out, trauma, and frustration, and the lack of jobs, shelter, and basic services (Rehn and Sirleaf 2002, quoting Lindsey 2002). In the aftermath of conflict, trauma that male combatants have suffered may be transformed into domestic violence. For example, in the countries of the former Yugoslavia, women working on SOS hotlines and in shelters believed that domestic and street violence increased—mainly against women—with men's return from fighting (Cockburn 1998). In post-conflict Kosovo, domestic violence seemed to become a growing problem given the number of survivors who sought shelter and the increased discussion of domestic violence (Astgeirsdottir 2002). Studies in Cambodia in the mid-1990s indicated that many women—up to 75 percent in one study—were domestic violence survivors, often at the hands of men who kept the small arms that they had used in the war (Rehn and Sirleaf 2002). Domestic violence affects not only the victim—it damages the fabric of society, creating fear in women's lives and socializing children into a culture of violence, which undermines social cohesion and transmits violence to the next generation.

Development Challenges: A Multidimensional Approach

Development efforts need to focus on the protection and recovery of GBV survivors. This requires the processing of experiences, breaking through the survivors' isolation and exclusion, and helping them to heal medically and mentally so that they can return to their daily activities. Multidimensional programming is required, including the active involvement of survivors and their communities, the health sector, social services, and the legal and security sectors. Positive

---

Box 3.1 Medica Zenica Project Aids Female GBV
Survivors in Bosnia and Herzegovina

In 1999, the Office of the High Commissioner for Human Rights
(OHCHR) in Bosnia and Herzegovina partnered with the anti-violence
NGO Medica Zenica on a pilot project to support GBV prevention and
prosecution by creating a community network of services for female
survivors of violence. Several international organizations, such as the
UN Mission in Bosnia and Herzegovina, OXFAM, and the Sarajevo-
based International Human Rights Law Group, worked with OHCHR
and Medica to reinforce sectoral links and to establish case management
protocols that involved the police, social and health services, and the judiciary. Activities included training, establishing a multisectoral task
force, and developing a community-based GBV awareness campaign
that was generally regarded as successful. Although cooperation among
NGOs, police, and the judiciary was initially problematic, the training
facilitated cross-sectoral coordination and resulted in more effective and
efficient services for women in the Zenica region (Ward 2002).

---

examples include the case of Medica Zenica (see box 3.1) in Bosnia
and Herzegovina (Cockburn 1998).

With GBV, it is critical to consider the different needs and requirements of women and men. GBV survivors and witnesses need to be
treated with the utmost sensitivity. Survivors are usually reluctant to
come forward because of shame, fear of reprisals by their family
and/or community, and potential damage to their reputation. Some
GBV cases will never be reported. Many survivors will never be
treated. Men should also be actively involved in preventing and addressing GBV [UN Fund for Population Activities (UNFPA) 2002].
Too little assistance has been provided to men to date.

Policy Options

GBV Awareness Raising

Raising awareness should ideally lead to acknowledging GBV in
conflict situations, addressing GBV in post-conflict reconstruction
(Kvinna till Kvinna 2001), and reducing GBV in the post-conflict
phase [International Office for Migration (IOM) 2002]. Sideris (2000)
cautions that "There is no substantial evidence to show that post-
war governments have taken the opportunity to use the obvious

Box 3.2 Anima Establishes a GBV Hotline

A 1997 survey in Gorazde, Bosnia, and Herzegovina revealed high domestic violence levels. The International Rescue Committee (IRC) responded by supporting the local NGO Anima's efforts to establish the first GBV hotline in the country. As part of the hotline promotion campaign, a local, well-known, media figure hosted regular radio programs where she acknowledged her personal exposure to domestic abuse. Anima also conducted outreach to local police and social services, facilitating sectoral coordination, and case management of women who reported abuse to the hotline. According to local police representatives, the media campaign resulted in an initial surge in police reporting, followed by a decrease in new and repeated domestic violence cases.

IRC's follow-up survey found that respondents who knew a domestic violence survivor had dropped from 55 to 36 percent and those agreeing that a man is entitled to hit his wife "if she does something wrong" dropped from 29 to 14 percent. Although Anima's hotline became a model for subsequent hotlines in other parts of Bosnia and Herzegovina, the hotline was shut down after two years because of a lack of funds. IRC's 1999 follow-up survey found strong support for the hotline among respondents; 95 percent thought that the hotline was a good idea, and 89 percent said that they would use the hotline if they were in an abusive relationship (Ward 2002).

sociopolitical content of sexual violence in war to challenge, in public forums, the sociocultural values and political practices that legitimate violence against women." Important entry points in GBV awareness campaigns are women's and men's sexual rights and control over their bodies and sexuality. The Gorazde case illustrates a successful approach to raising GBV awareness (see box 3.2).

An important aspect of effective awareness campaigns is to involve men, from both the general public and from occupational groups involved in managing the problem. Examples include the White Ribbon Campaign in Kosovo, seminars on GBV against women in connection with the UN Mission in Kosovo (UNMIK), and the activities of the Association of Men Against Violence in Nicaragua (see box 3.3).

A recent UN Development Fund for Women (UNIFEM) report provides an overview of successful communication strategies and media materials to raise awareness and combat violence against women. The strategies and materials focus on domestic violence, sexual assaults such as rape and sexual abuse, trafficking, commercial sexual exploitation, HIV/AIDS, and violence (UNIFEM 2001; UNDP 2003).

Box 3.3 Different Methods Are Used to Raise GBV
Awareness among Men

On the International Day to Eliminate Violence Against Women (November 25), women's organizations in Kosovo made white ribbons for the White Ribbon Campaign. This campaign started in Canada, is now active in over 30 countries, and is the largest global effort to engage men in ending violence against women. A white ribbon is a pledge never to commit, condone, or remain silent about violence against women. The local radio station supported the campaign through public announcements, by attending the events, and producing a live radio show.[20]

The IRC and the Wellness Center Team in the Pejë/Pec region conducted seminars on violence against women. The team gave a presentation on domestic violence in relation to UNMIK. Four attendees were policemen from the Pejë/Pec region. After the seminar, the IRC Wellness Team was requested to give training on domestic violence to the local police. There were 46 local police attendees, 14 of them women.

In Nicaragua, the Association of Men Against Violence was founded in 1993 and in 2000 became a national association to unite local groups. The association's goal is to reduce violence against women by confronting masculinity and aggression issues. It seeks to educate and sensitize men regarding patriarchal traditions, gender equality, power, and GBV. It offers training workshops on *machismo* and violence, promotes alliances with women's groups, and participates in public awareness campaigns that address masculinity and violence issues (Ward 2002).

In India, for example, the government made gender sensitization training mandatory for police officers; in Croatia, trade unions adopted policies against sexual harassment and filed the first criminal charges; and laws against domestic violence were passed in Latin America. However, the Reproductive Health for Refugees Consortium cautions on the need for sensitivity and delivering results to GBV survivors (see box 3.4).

Psychological Assistance to GBV Survivors

Following conflict, a large part of the population is likely to show post-traumatic stress. Long after the conflict is over, many people still struggle with psychosocial isolation (e.g., Brittain 2002) and difficulties in getting 'back on track' (e.g., Kvinna till Kvinna 2002). There is a clear need for long-term psychological assistance for conflict survivors in general and for GBV survivors in particular. Regarding

---

Box 3.4 Is There Too Much Research and
           Not Enough Action?

The international community responded to the rape of thousands of
women in Bosnia with scores of programs and initiatives, many of
which frustrated and angered the very women that they were intended
to help. "I am sick of the media and everyone coming here and asking
us to talk about our experiences of rape," said one woman. In Rwanda,
where the extraordinary levels of violence during the genocide included
the rape and brutalizing of women, responses were similar. "We talked
to the researchers who came here and they wrote about us," remarked
one woman, as a small group of women nodded their heads in assent,
"What good did that do us? It did nothing to help us."

Aid workers and others documenting violence against women need
to explain the purpose of their questions, the results they expect from
the interviews, and the impact it might or might not have on those in-
terviewed (Forced Migration 1997 Web site).

---

the latter, psychological counseling for all the actors involved (survivors, survivors' families, witnesses, and perpetrators) is increasingly
becoming a standard component of humanitarian and post-conflict rehabilitation efforts. And while the literature reviewed accepts that
agencies should build on and support local capacities for counseling
GBV survivors [World Health Organization (WHO) 1996, 2000; Vann
2002], it does not elaborate on the gender dimensions. Further analysis is required to assess how local mental recovery processes impact
male and female GBV survivors. Gender-specific factors include the
presence of male and female counselors, the openness of local counselors to GBV cases, and the chances that complaints will be addressed. A good example of local counseling is the Sierra Leone
Women's Forum. The forum popularized counseling GBV survivors,
which was previously unavailable in the country, and adapted Western
therapeutic models to local practices by including storytelling,
proverbs, and singing in the treatment (Ward 2002).

Lessons and best practices identified in the literature include the
following:[21]

- Adapt counseling techniques to local cultures, customs, and needs
  of GBV survivors (ICRC 2001; Save the Children 2003). This requires cooperating not only with health facilities and NGOs, but
  also with local traditional counselors (WHO 2000). However,

agencies must remain critical of traditional practices that could be harmful or dangerous to survivors (WHO 1996), and they should note that local counseling preferences differ (Vann 2002).[22]

- Provide psychological assistance to women and men. View men not only as GBV perpetrators, but also as survivors or as empowered bystanders who can confront abusive peers.

- In addition to one-to-one counseling for women, men, and children, adopt a community-based approach to psychosocial recovery. Community-based approaches can reach more people than individual approaches, while facilitating the restoration of family networks and support structures and thereby improving community cohesion and healing (WHO 2000). It is essential to include the participation of sufficient numbers of female community leaders in community-based approaches. Separate women's and men's self-help groups may also be needed [e.g., UN High Commissioner for Refugees (UNHCR) 2003].

- Change attitudes by referring to victims as survivors and heroes and provide counseling under conditions that the survivor determines (for example, with confidentiality, at the time he or she wants to speak).

- Secure the safety of survivors and witnesses and protect them from further exploitation and abuse.

- Set up hotlines and reception centers for survivors and ensure that such centers are not immediately identifiable to the community as being associated with sexual violence and other gender discrimination issues (see box 3.5).

- Respect confidentiality but bear in mind that, the more GBV is treated confidentially, particularly domestic violence, the more the public will assume that violence is not happening or that violence is acceptable and the abuser can be excused.

- Form counseling teams that include a human rights worker and a psychosocial worker who are trained to work together to interview victims with sensitivity.

- Interview survivors only once, avoiding the need to subject them to repeated interviews, but ensure that follow-up treatment is available and combine psychosocial support with medical and economic assistance.

Medical Assistance to GBV Survivors

Providing medical assistance to GBV survivors should be of concern not only to local health care agencies but also to other actors such as the police and social welfare services. It is vital that all these agencies

---

Box 3.5 IRC's Tanzania GBV Program Helps Burundian
Female Refugees

IRC's Tanzania GBV Program has served Burundian refugees in western
Tanzania since late 1996. Using a needs assessment, the program decided to establish a 24-hour support service for GBV survivors. In each
of four refugee camps, it created a drop-in center at a safe and friendly
location where women regularly gathered, such as near the maternity
wards and maternal and health clinics in the camps. This helped survivors avoid being identified or stigmatized for seeking assistance and
allowed women to feel safe and assured of confidentiality. Because the
drop-in centers offered a range of gynecological and other health services in addition to addressing GBV problems, people could not assume
that every woman who came in was a GBV survivor. The center staff met
women's medical and protection needs, provided psychosocial counseling on how to continue living in the community, and facilitated medical
examinations and treatment for trauma, STDs such as HIV/AIDS, and
pregnancy. They also offered referrals to social workers when a woman
wished to apply for family separation and assisted those intending to
take legal action.[23]

---

have an appropriate understanding of GBV and an adequate referral
system at their disposal to inform survivors where to seek assistance.
This section focuses on health sector workers as they tend to be the
first contact point for survivors and are essential in breaking the
silence around GBV [Institute for Security Studies (ISS) 2002].

External support can help strengthen local health workers' capacity
to manage GBV. Agencies such as WHO, UNHCR, and UNFPA have
amassed substantial experience in the provision of medical assistance
to GBV survivors. For example, they developed and field-tested man-
uals on managing reproductive health, including sexual health in
emergencies (WHO/UNFPA/UNHCR 1999; WHO 2000), and rape
survivors (WHO/UNHCR 2002). They have practical guidelines to
formulate laws on reproductive health, including sexual health (WHO
2001, 2002). Although most of their experiences relate to emergency
operations, they also provide useful lessons and best practices to
strengthen local health services, as detailed below:

- Identify and protect individuals or groups that may be particularly
  at risk from GBV and address their protection and assistance

needs (WHO/UNFPA/UNHCR 1999). Agencies can support sending women and girls to safer locations or encourage them to seek safety in numbers (Human Rights Watch 2002). ICRC encourages camps for refugees and IDPs to take practical measures such as fencing off women's quarters (ICRC 2001). ICRC delegates also visit GBV survivors or their families and confidentially record their testimonies; based on the agreement of the survivors, relevant authorities are requested to put an end to the violations or to investigate allegations (ICRC 2001).

- Improve survivors' access to information especially on the availability of services.
- Raise the awareness of health workers, health ministries, and other relevant actors on the need for basic health care and reproductive health care throughout conflict and adapt existing health services accordingly (WHO 2000; ICRC 2001; WHO/UNHCR 2002).
- Provide additional training to health workers and other relevant actors to investigate and respond sensitively to GBV cases, including knowing when to refer GBV survivors to specialized agencies.
- Ensure the presence of a same-sex health worker (and translator) for medical examinations (WHO 1999, 2001).
- Support staff working with violence survivors, since they may also suffer distress when providing treatment.

In all the issues outlined above, high HIV/AIDS prevalence rates among GBV survivors should be considered explicitly. In addition to information and awareness, agencies should consider additional steps, such as confidential testing for HIV/AIDS or other STDs. By developing internal protocols and measures, agencies can better protect staff against abuse and the sexual exploitation of local women and men (see box 3.6).

Institutional Capacity

To enforce regulations that are sensitive to GBV, it is important that institutions such as the judiciary, the welfare system, and police participate in the process (legal protection against GBV is discussed in chapter 6, below). As these institutions are responsible for implementing regulations, they often need guidance and training. Training should include general gender issues and gender equality, GBV awareness, working with GBV survivors, and identification and punishment of

Box 3.6 Peace Operations in Cambodia Had Negative
        Social Impacts

In Cambodia in the early 1990s, a number of problems arose concerning the behavior of UN troops and security personnel and their relations
with host populations. The influx of troops and other foreigners contributed to an increase in prostitution. While this was to be expected,
the scale of the phenomenon was not. Neither was the ten-fold increase
in the incidence of HIV/AIDS infection in 1992. The growth of the rest-
and-recreation industry impacted not only women but children as well.
There is evidence that children were increasingly used in the sex industry, partly to minimize the perceived risk to clients of becoming infected
with HIV/AIDS or other diseases. Phnom Penh's "attractions," when
combined with a decline in the education system and the needs of many
families to mobilize all potential earners, fueled a growth in the number
of street children.

In peacekeeping operations, much stricter guidelines governing the
recruitment, briefing, and training of peacekeeping and professional
personnel are needed. Special attention should be given to the question
of social relations with host populations to prevent foreign troops from
sexually exploiting local women, to the provision of on-base recreation
facilities, and to the possibility of testing peacekeeping forces for
HIV/AIDS when they enter and leave the country.[24]

GBV perpetrators.[25] In Albania, for example, the Organization for
Security and Economic Cooperation in Europe (OSCE), in cooperation
with IOM, developed a training curriculum on human rights, gender
equality, and GBV and integrated it into the police academy curriculum. Male police trainers and women's NGOs proved to be effective
trainers and helped the police to recognize and handle trafficking in
women and domestic violence.[26] GBV was presented as a human rights
issue, and the training showed how GBV contravened international
conventions and the state's responsibilities (OSCE 2001).

In addition to training, agencies have successfully applied other
forms of institutional capacity building to achieve the following results:

- Promote coordination between the judiciary, NGOs, the police,
  and other law-enforcing bodies to raise awareness, identify
  obstacles, and devise innovative ways of anticipating violence
  (OSCE 2001).
- Establish a mutual referral system between agencies to direct
  survivors to the right place for assistance.

- Establish special units within the police, judiciary, and immigration agencies that specifically address trafficking, domestic violence, and sexual assault during and after conflict (UNFPA 2002; International Alert 2002). In Sierra Leone a female police officer took the initiative to address some of the reporting challenges that GBV survivors face. With the support and guidance of a UN Mission British officer in Sierra Leone, she established a domestic violence police unit, created protocols and training to respond to survivors of rape and domestic violence, and started collecting police report data on violence against women (Ward 2002).
- Ensure that police officers do not serve as counselors or mediators, but rather serve to link survivors to support structures. If the police are involved in counseling, it may confuse the police's role in the community and create the impression that the violence is not serious enough to warrant a criminal justice system intervention (OSCE 2001).
- Encourage more equal recruitment of women and men in the police, judiciary, and related agencies, which may increase interest in and sensitivity to GBV.
- Implement regimes and practices to regulate and monitor agencies that are frequently linked with the *modus operandi* of trafficking for sexual exploitation (e.g., bridal, tourist, escort, *au pair,* or adoption agencies).[27]

These institution-building options may not only improve performance, but also contribute to a greater sensitivity and attention by the police, judiciary, and other relevant institutions regarding general gender issues. As such, they can be good starting points for gender-sensitizing the institutions.

Increased Attention for Male GBV Survivors

While it is increasingly recognized that men are also GBV survivors in conflict-affected areas, this acknowledgment has not been translated into policies to address male victims. A number of authors point out that sexual violence against men must be understood as a gendered act that is designed to "reduce" men to the status of women (e.g., Cockburn 1998; El-Bushra and Piza-Lopez 1993; Nordang 2002; and Turshen 1998).[28] Assistance for male survivors is often absent, which sometimes has led male victims to approach women's groups for counseling, as was the case in Kosovo and Serbia.[29] In essence, the initial psychological, medical, legal, and institutional responses to male GBV survivors may be the same as for female survivors. A counselor, doctor, protection officer, and interpreter of the same sex should see them, if possible. Male staff should receive training in how to respond to the needs of male GBV survivors (WHO 2000). However, psychological counselors may need to take into account that male GBV survivors are even less likely than women to report their experiences (WHO/UNHCR 2002). Particularly in societies where men are discouraged from talking about their emotions, they may find it even more difficult than women to acknowledge what has happened to them. For these reasons, there is probably considerable underreporting of sexual violence against males (WHO 2000). Moreover, doctors should investigate the specific physical harm done to males, which obviously differs from that done to women (WHO/UNHCR 2002), and legal specialists should ensure that women and men have equal legal protection against GBV. Although networks and programs exist to protect females who were sexually attacked, there is rarely anything comparable for male survivors. In some countries, the legal definition of rape applies only to women.

Finally, combating GBV will not be effective without changing the culture of violence and providing alternatives for militarized masculinities in conflict-affected countries. As long as violence is tolerated and social norms and values do not condemn such violence, policy changes will have only minimal impact. Although it is a huge challenge, agencies need to consider how to approach such militarized societies and attitudes and break the continuum of violence.

CHAPTER 4

Gender and Formal
Peace Processes

Overview

STARTING FROM THE PERSPECTIVE THAT women and men can be as effective in promoting peace as in promoting war and conflict, this chapter focuses on women's and men's positions in formal peace processes throughout conflict. It analyzes their roles in democratization processes, elections, and political processes during and after conflict.

Most political institutions in conflict and nonconflict societies tend to perpetuate an exclusionary attitude and culture toward women. As a result, compared to men relatively few women become involved in formal peace processes during and after conflict. Beyond this quantitative *difference,* there is a qualitative difference; women are likely to make a different contribution to the peace process. When compared to men, women are more likely to put gender issues on the agenda, introduce other conflict experiences, and set different priorities for peace building and rehabilitation, and they may bridge political divides better. Women's increased participation may also generate wider public support for the peace accords. However, one should avoid the view that all female politicians are gender-sensitive, while all male politicians are not.

Regarding gender-role *changes,* additional analysis is needed to determine whether women's participation in formal political processes increases during conflict. Such analysis needs to focus on how conducive factors (i.e., a decrease in stereotypical gender divisions of labor and the absence of males) and impeding factors (i.e., an increase in domestic burdens and the absence of functioning political bodies) shape women's opportunities for political participation during conflict. Since prevailing social structures and gender divisions tend to accompany the return of peace, many women have to retreat from political and public life. This dip in female participation may be temporary and is often reversed due to external pressure to establish democratic systems and open political space for women.

The political processes during conflict and post-conflict may offer possibilities for greater gender balance. Peace talks, democratization processes, and elections are looked upon as embodying and bringing positive changes. The *key development challenge* is to use the momentum to focus attention on gender-equality issues and to increase the involvement of women and other marginalized groups in the peace process.

To incorporate gender equality into peace accords, policy options include:

- Organizing training and information-sharing events for politicians already in office or those involved in the peace talks;
- Developing wider processes of political consultation or representation, for example, with women's organizations;
- Increasing the number of female politicians by training women to run for political office, from the village to the parliamentary level;
- Fostering discussion within public and political bodies about women's involvement;
- Setting legislative or party quotas to ensure a minimum number of female candidates; and
- Establishing indicators to assess the influence of female and male politicians on political outcomes and the political culture and process.

Gender Roles in the Peace Process

While women are often active in informal peace processes, they are largely absent from formal peace processes. As defined by the UN, formal peace processes include early warning, preventive diplomacy, conflict prevention, peacemaking, peace-building, and global disarmament; they involve activities such as conflict resolution, peace negotiations, reconciliation, infrastructure reconstruction, and provision of humanitarian aid (adapted from Porter 2003). The UN argues that women need to be included in formal peace processes to build greater post-conflict gender balance and a more inclusive peace. Women's participation in the peace process and mainstreaming their involvement into the peace accords lay the groundwork for engendering post-conflict reconstruction and rehabilitation (Sheckler 2002). At the same time, conflict may increase opportunities for more gender-balanced political participation, but support is needed to sustain these changes after conflict. Chapter 5 discusses women's participation in informal peace processes. Although the Bank is precluded by its mandate from intervening or directly participating in political processes or peace negotiations, it needs to understand these processes and their implications for effective post-conflict recovery efforts.

Politics, the state, nationalism, and the army are fundamentally masculine notions. They are characterized by patriarchal practices and values that are not easily changed (Wilford and Miller 1998). Meintjes (1998) describes how in South Africa women have been identified as "mothers of the nation." However, women's practical involvement as well as the ideological discourse employed in defining the sphere of their actions centered on motherhood, responsibility for children, and protection of the family—the national discourse was framed within patriarchal boundaries.

Whether in conflict or nonconflict situations, most political institutions tend to exclude women. As a result, many women choose to work outside formal politics, with various CSOs, and/or with political parties that advocate social and political change (UNDP 2003). So it is not surprising that, compared to men, relatively few women become involved in formal peace processes, from negotiations that often begin in the midst of conflict and continue through the various phases of the transition to peace (Naraghi Anderlini 2000). These processes tend to remain male-dominated; women are underrepresented at all levels, including in international agencies supporting peace negotiations, in negotiation teams representing the warring parties, and in other institutions invited to the negotiation table (Byrne 1996; Sörensen 1998; Kvinna till Kvinna 2000; Porter 2003).[30] Barnes (2002) refers to an "elite pact-making approach" by which those willing to use power divide the spoils without the participation of society at large. Porter (2003) refers to a strong belief that those who take up arms must stop the conflict by sitting at the negotiating table. This approach may help to end violent conflict, but it does not necessarily provide the best basis for rebuilding society. Inclusion of all social groups fosters the pluralism that is necessary to develop a more inclusive, stable, and participatory post-conflict polity.

Because it is precisely at the peace accords where the foundations for a future society are often set, this is where important gender issues should be addressed and where a gender perspective on peace should be incorporated (Cock 2001). Whereas it may be hard to achieve gender equality in every component of the peace accords and post-conflict political reconciliation processes—particularly if gender balance was largely absent in the pre-conflict phase—efforts are needed to address

gender issues to the extent possible. Gender issues that could be incorporated in peace accords include: human rights provisions in new constitutions, equal participation in elections, participation of women and
men in decisionmaking, laws against GBV, prosecution of GBV perpetrators, special measures to set up gender-sensitive police forces and
other key institutions, and greater gender balance in inheritance rights
and access to land, property, housing, and credit (UN 2002). Ideally,
such issues will not be addressed exclusively in the peace accords, but
they will also be elaborated in the political and legal processes that
result from the peace accords.

What difference could increased female participation make in the
peace process and political reconciliation? For example, could it be assumed that greater participation of women at the Dayton Talks or in
Sierra Leone would have put the equal rights and needs of women and
men more prominently on the agenda? Naraghi Anderlini (2000)
shows that women's increased participation (as politicians, informants, negotiators, or representatives) enhances the chance that major
gender issues will be discussed during peace talks and incorporated in
peace accords. Women's contribution to conflict resolution and peace
building is regarded as generally positive (Naraghi Anderlini 2000; UN
2002; Rehn and Sirleaf 2002). Naraghi Anderlini (2000) finds that, in
addition to placing gender issues more frequently on the peace agenda
than men, women often introduce other conflict experiences and set
different priorities for peace-building and rehabilitation. They tend to
be the sole voices speaking out for women's rights and concerns, often
forging coalitions based on women's shared interests that transcend
political, ethnic, and religious differences (see box 4.1), and bringing
a better understanding of social justice and gender inequality to
peace negotiations. They are often regarded as less threatening to the
established order, thus having more freedom of action. Although there
has been little systematic research, anecdotal evidence suggests that
women may unite around such issues as motherhood or on the basis of
their family responsibilities, whereas such 'bridging' elements seem less
important for men. Addressing women's concerns need not be equated
with notions of feminism, but as the primary caretakers, women tend
to prioritize education, health, nutrition, childcare, and human welfare
needs. Without a voice, women's concerns are neither prioritized nor
resourced (Porter 2003).

Women's participation in peace talks can also widen the popular
mandate for peace and lead to concrete measures, such as: ministries
for gender equality and women's affairs (Afghanistan), separate units
within ministries to address gender issues (Liberia), equal rights to
vote and participate in political processes (Cambodia), and changed

---

Box 4.1 Building Women's Alliances in Burundi, Liberia, and Northern Ireland

Forming women's alliances can be a difficult process, particularly when they are divided along political and identity lines (El-Bushra 2003). Nevertheless, in a number of cases women have managed to form coalitions that bridge deep political, ethnic, and religious divides on the basis of shared interests. In protracted conflicts such as in Northern Ireland, women collaborated on cross-community programs relating to childcare, health, and microenterprises. In Liberia, members of the Liberian Women's Initiative—which was open to all women regardless of ethnic, social, or religious background—became informants during the regional peace talks and acted as monitors of commitments made (Naraghi Anderlini 2000). As a result of extensive advocacy, women in Burundi were able to unite across ethnic, political, and class backgrounds and developed a clear agenda and joint recommendations, many of which were included in the peace agreement (UN 2002).

---

attitudes to women's leadership and decisionmaking capacities (Northern Ireland) (Naraghi Anderlini 2000). Women's participation in the peace talks in Guatemala (1991–96) resulted in efforts to ensure more equal access to land and credit, a special health program for women and girls, a family reunification program, legislation penalizing sexual harassment, and the creation of the National Women's Forum and the Office for the Defense of Indigenous Women (UN 2002).

It should not be assumed *a priori,* however, that women's presence in the peace process will guarantee that gender equality issues will be on the agenda. Although nearly one-third of FMLN (Farabundo Martí National Liberation Front) negotiators were women, gender equality was not incorporated in El Salvador's peace agreements, which even included some discriminatory provisions against women (UN 2002). However, as noted in boxes 4.2 and 7.3, below, women's presence in the peace process did make a difference. Although women may not always support opportunities for other women, in general, they are still the main proponents of agendas that include gender (Naraghi Anderlini 2000). Research from Scandinavia shows that it is mostly female politicians who place women's position in society issues on the formal political agenda (Dahlerup 2001). Ensuring more balanced gender representation in the peace process is likely to increase the chances that key gender issues will be addressed in peace accords. Since not all

---

Box 4.2 Women Participated in El Salvador's
Peace Negotiations

High-ranking women in the FMLN and Salvadoran government participated in all phases of the peace negotiations. While in the early stages
they regarded themselves as official party negotiators—"not as representatives of a women's movement"—their presence nonetheless had an
important effect on the outcome. In the words of Ana Guadalupe
Martínez, a high-ranking FMLN official, women in the negotiations
were well respected, but "not as a woman, but as a representative of a
powerful armed group" (Conaway and Martínez 2004). With hind-
sight, many female FMLN fighters regret their lack of gender awareness
during the peace process. But while they did not address concerns specific to women, their presence in the negotiations made a significant difference, particularly regarding reintegration benefits. As Nidia Díaz, a
former FMLN *comandante,* recalls: "In negotiating, when the time
came to discuss the concept of beneficiaries, it was understood in our
heads that women would participate, but that wasn't [written] specifically. And we had problems because when the lists of beneficiaries were
formulated, members of the [negotiating] team did not specifically put
down the names of women. It was a very serious problem that we had
later because only the men were thought of as beneficiaries, and we had
to return to re-do lists. . . . " (Conaway and Martínez 2004).

---

women and men can be officially represented in the peace process,
wider processes of societal consultation are important for inclusive
peace processes.

Dynamics: Struggling for Participation

Women's roles in public and social life generally expand during conflict. This may be shaped, for example, by a decrease in stereotypical
gender divisions of labor, the absence of males, or women's support
for peace processes. Kumar (2001) notes that during conflict a number
of women took charge of political institutions in El Salvador, and that
33 out of 262 mayors elected during 1985–88 were women. Whether
this represents a more general trend is difficult to judge due to the absence of comparative data, which suggests the need for additional research. It may be that existing barriers are often too strong in the early
phases of conflict to encourage women's political participation or that
their participation may be constrained by the extra domestic burdens

they face. In addition, in many conflict situations there is hardly a functioning representative government or parliament where women could become politically active. Another limitation may be of a qualitative nature. Even when political systems continue to function, the women's role often remains marginal or is co-opted by political players in the name of supporting the war effort. Women's activities are often relegated to special women's wings of political parties or sidelined in independent women's and feminist groups that fail to have a significant impact on mainstream politics and decisionmaking.

Greater political participation during conflict may also be temporary [Norwegian Institute of International Affairs (NUPI) 2001]. As Karame noted, there seems to be no connection between women's political agency during conflict and their participation in national postconflict decisionmaking processes (Bouta and Frerks 2002, quoting Karame 1999). The War-Torn Societies Project (WSP) notes that "Once peace returns, traditional social structures and gender divisions often return also. These may remove women from the positions of responsibility they assumed during times of war and return them to more traditional roles. This not only deals a blow to social and economic survival strategies and informal economic networks, but becomes the source of new tensions." (WSP Web site.) Bop (2001) states that, despite the rights won during conflict, women's loss of opportunities to exercise political and social leadership immediately after conflict is among the most extreme and long-lasting of their losses.

Similarly, El-Bushra (2003) indicates that women managed to play political roles at the community and national levels during conflict in countries such as Sudan and Uganda, but that such gender changes at the micro level are often not accompanied by corresponding changes in political or organizational influence, and they do not fundamentally alter patriarchal ideologies. In Algeria, women were directly prevented from running in the 1990 elections (Sörensen 1998, quoting Byrne 1996). In other cases—Bosnia and Herzegovina, Cambodia, and Guatemala—women had to leave the political arena immediately after the conflict, although the reasons are not fully understood. As Bop (2001) remarks in the African context: "No systematic analysis has yet explained why African women have lost the leadership positions they had previously won." Some factors likely include reintroduction of the traditional social and political order existing before the conflict, war fatigue that grips some women leaders, or—perhaps more significant— men seeking to reassert their authority (Kumar 2001). It could also be explained by the fact that while changes in gender *roles* often do take place, the ideological basis underpinning gender *relations* may remain largely unchanged (El-Bushra et al. 2002).

Box 4.3 Women's Post-Conflict Political Participation
Increases over Time

Country case studies in Bosnia and Herzegovina, Cambodia, El
Salvador, Georgia, Guatemala, and Rwanda show how the retreat of
women from public and political life after conflict is visible in post-
conflict elections to establish democratic governments. Although women
made up at least half of the electorate, they were only marginally represented initially in post-conflict national legislatures. Five women were
elected to the National Assembly in Cambodia, representing only 6 percent of elected representatives. In Guatemala, women occupied only
7.5 percent of seats in parliament. In Bosnia and Herzegovina, there was
only one woman in the 42-member House of Representatives. In El
Salvador and Mozambique, women held 11 percent and 25 percent of
the seats, respectively.

After an initial dip in the first post-conflict elections, however, the
percentage of women elected in the national legislatures of Bosnia and
Herzegovina, Cambodia, El Salvador, and Georgia showed an upward
trend in subsequent elections, arguably influenced by donor pressure.

A more recent tabulation of the percentage of women in parliament
(lower house or single house) shows that, remarkably, Rwanda, with
49 percent women, ranks first among 176 countries, well ahead of
Nordic countries and The Netherlands. Post-conflict countries ranked
among the top 50 include: Mozambique (30 percent), Timor-Leste
(26 percent), Uganda (25 percent), Eritrea (22 percent), Nicaragua (21 percent), and Burundi (18 percent) (Inter-Parliamentary Union Web site
2004).

Women's representation in national ministries and local elections
also improved over time. The percentage of female city counselors in El
Salvador increased from only 3 percent during the conflict to 14 percent
in the 1993 elections and almost doubled by the 1999 elections (Kumar
2001). In Rwanda, women held nine ministerial positions in 1994 and
five in 1998, but the number jumped to 26 by 2002—in no small part
because of explicit donor pressure (Weill 2003).

On a more positive note, this dip in female political participation at
the end of a conflict can be of a short nature (see box 4.3). The international community present in the post-conflict phase increasingly
advocates equal participation by women and men. The pressure to establish democratic systems opens up new political space for women
and women's organizations to become publicly and politically active.

Development Challenges: Gender-Sensitizing
the Political Process

There is growing recognition that economic and political participation cannot be separated (Hamadeh-Banerjee 2000) and that effective development requires greater gender balance in power sharing (Kumar 2001). The political processes during conflict and post-conflict may offer possibilities to encourage greater gender balance in political power. Peace talks, democratization processes, and elections can provide opportunities to usher in positive changes. Article 1 of UN Security Council (UNSC) Resolution 1325 urges states to ensure increased women's representation at all decisionmaking levels in national, regional, and international institutions and mechanisms for the prevention, management, and resolution of conflict, while Article 8 calls on all actors to adopt a gender perspective when negotiating and implementing peace agreements (UNSC 2000).

Although the relationship between conflict, peace, and democracy is multifaceted and partly contested, the "democratic peace" thesis argues that democracies do not fight one another. Fukuyama (1998) observes that developed democracies also tend to be more feminized than authoritarian states: "It should therefore surprise no one that the historically unprecedented shift in the sexual basis of politics should lead to a change in international relations." This observation is in line with findings that increased gender equality results in less belligerent foreign policy behavior, as women are considered less aggressive and driven by values such as interdependence and egalitarianism. In Caprioli's (2000) quantitative analysis, political, social, and economic measures of gender equality predict a state's international militarism, i.e., greater gender equality reduces the likelihood that a state will attack its neighbors. In a more recent analysis undertaken for the World Bank, Caprioli (2003) seeks to determine whether gender inequality is also a meaningful predictor of intrastate conflict. She hypothesizes that gender inequality should have a dual impact on intrastate conflict—first, as a manifestation of structural and cultural violence, it can lead to heightened social violence, and second, it facilitates a nationalist call to arms. She finds that gender inequality increases the likelihood that a state will experience internal conflict—states with high fertility rates, taken as a proxy for gender inequality,[31] are twice as likely to experience internal conflict as low-fertility ones; 88 percent of the PRIO/Uppsala[32]-coded internal conflicts are within states with a fertility rate over 3.0.

Policy Options

Incorporating Gender Equality into Peace Accords and Political Rehabilitation Activities

Addressing gender equality in the political arena is not exclusively the task of women, but also that of men. It is not solely the responsibility of politicians, but also of political observers, representatives, civil servants, and other political actors. Gender issues should not only be addressed at the national level, but also in governance structures at the regional and community levels. Policy options include:

- *Gender awareness training.* Training and information sharing with women and men in office on relevant gender issues may increase their gender sensitivity (OSCE 2001; GTZ 2001). Women's organizations can be instrumental in conducting training courses and awareness campaigns (see box 4.4). However, the

---

Box 4.4 A "Women Can Do It" Campaign Unfolds in Southeastern Europe

The Stability Pact for Southeastern Europe's Gender Task Force (GTF) implemented a "Women Can Do It" Campaign. The Norwegian Labor Party developed the campaign in the early 1980s to encourage the Party's female politicians to take gender issues more seriously. The program was first adapted to the needs of social democratic women in transition countries, adjusted in 1999 to the needs of (future) female politicians of all political parties in Bosnia and Herzegovina, and recently introduced in Croatia, Montenegro, and Serbia. The campaign aims to stimulate women's participation in political life and to encourage women to take gender issues into account. Training was developed to help women understand that they have different qualities and priorities from men and that they have the right and the duty to bring these into mainstream politics. Training tried to help them overcome male dominance, by focusing on skills such as how to work in politics, public speaking, preparing for political work, networking, and lobbying.

In 2001, the GTF determined that these training sessions were not enough. Even when women entered political life, they were still a small minority, lacked visibility, and found it difficult to be heard. So the GTF developed a second module to empower women within their own political parties. In 2002, the GTF trained nearly all the women's groups in parliamentary parties in Southeastern Europe.[33] To date, no systematic evaluation has been undertaken of the results.

Box 4.5 Burundi's Peace Process Incorporates Gender
and Women's Issues

A high-profile delegation of female politicians from several African countries was invited to the peace negotiations in Burundi to speak about gender and women's issues. The 19 parties were briefed on the way in which gender could be related to the peace process. They discussed issues such as drafting a constitution, electoral systems, and war crimes. An All-Party Burundi Women's Conference was subsequently held to discuss and formulate recommendations to include the protection of women and women's rights in the peace accords. Recommendations were distributed to the parties and discussed in negotiations; 23 of the recommendations were incorporated in the final peace accords, including the legalization of women's right to inherit land and property and girls' access to education (NUPI 2001).

---

limitation of this approach is that it focuses exclusively on women and men in office. As not all women and men, minorities, and parties manage to hold office or are involved in formal peace talks, Track II negotiations, other political processes, and/or wider processes of political consultation are needed to ensure that these groups are consulted about their needs and interests.

- *Develop wider processes of political consultation or representation.* Regarding gender equality, wider consultation processes with civil society organizations, particularly women's organizations, should be supported (Byrne 1996; UN 2002). Women's organizations usually have a good understanding of which gender issues should be addressed (see box 4.5). International agencies should encourage broad consultations in formal political processes during and after conflict. While monitoring the impact of such consultative processes on the contents of peace accords is important, implementation of the accords is key. In combination with measures to gender sensitize women and men in political office, this will increase the chance that gender issues are seriously considered in peace accords and the post-conflict political processes.

Equal Participation in Decisionmaking Structures and Elections

Because more men than women have the education, training, and self-confidence to operate in the political arena, educational and training activities should target women. To encourage well-trained and qualified

---

Box 4.6 Cambodian Women's NGOs Train Successful
Women Political Candidates

In February 2002, Cambodia held its first democratically contested
commune elections in three decades. A total of 75,244 candidates ran in
the 1,621 commune constituencies; of these candidates, 11,853 were
women (16 percent of all candidates). Aided by Asia Foundation
Bangkok staff, women's NGOs organized an initial training of trainers
session. The trainers then organized 124 workshops across the country,
providing training for 5,527 women, of whom 60 percent registered as
candidates; of these candidates, 900 were elected, compared to only
10 countrywide in the past. In addition, the Women for Prosperity NGO
undertook a donor-supported media and communication campaign to
promote female candidates on a nonpartisan basis.[34]

---

female candidates to enter politics, affirmative action is an option
(GTZ 2001) at the local, national, and regional levels for candidates,
officials, voters, and political activists (NUPI 2001). Since there is no
shortcut to integrating women and men into decisionmaking
processes, a long-term development perspective is needed. Policy
options must go beyond raw numbers to encompass the complex relationship of power, poverty, and participation (UNDP 2000). Policy
options include the following:

• *Train and recruit women and men to stand as candidates for
  formal political office in village councils, provincial legislatures,
  and national parliaments during and after conflict* [United States
  Agency for International Development (USAID) 2000]. International organizations can assist women to run as candidates in
  elections (see box 4.6), although finding suitable female candidates is often a challenge. An option may be to focus on women
  who have had little pre-conflict political experience or training,
  but have gained some political experience during conflict (NUPI
  2001). They need training to compensate for their lack of
  broader political experience and to increase their knowledge on
  a range of political topics that are pertinent in nonconflict situations. Such training may also reduce women's post-conflict
  dropout rate from politics. Another option is to target women
  who have substantial experience in informal processes. They may
  have a solid basis for entering formal processes, but their experiences are often not directly applicable to the formal political

arena (UN 2002). Another possibility is to focus on young women and men, who are probably less conditioned by gendered roles and more open to political change and to more balanced gender participation in politics (Hamadeh-Banerjee 2000).

- *Foster public and governmental discussions on the involvement of women and men in the political process.* Issues to stress include:
  - Opening informal and formal politics to men and women (i.e., not linking women exclusively to informal politics and men to formal politics), as they can be active in both fields;
  - Avoiding stereotyping female candidates and executive appointees that marginalize them to work in the softer areas of government, such as health and education, and away from the power-oriented portfolios, such as public works, trade, finance, and defense; and
  - Stressing women's and men's equal rights to register, vote, be nominated by a political party, get elected, be appointed to executive office, and hold any portfolio (Sörensen 1998; OSCE 2001).
- *Quotas.* Different quota systems in legislatures or political parties can ensure more balanced gender participation. Some countries reserve parliamentary seats for women or their electoral law decrees that a percentage (say, 30 percent) of candidates must be women or that 5 out of the first 15 names on party lists must be women. Sometimes the media is used or transport is provided to promote voting by women. Lessons include:
  - Quotas must be seen as temporary and a first step on the path to greater gender balance—a practical and symbolic measure to support women's leadership.
  - Quotas may need to be complemented by long-term efforts to address the socioeconomic constraints that affect women's participation in the political process (Rehn and Sirleaf 2002).
  - Quota systems should not disregard the capacity of candidates and should consider job requirements and women's and men's capacity to match them. A drawback of quotas is that if there are insufficient female candidates, parties may compromise quality for numbers.
  - Quota systems are more effective if they are combined with public awareness campaigns, networking between female politicians, education, and training (Kvinna till Kvinna 2001. NUPI 2001) (see box 4.7).
  - Quota systems generally aim at 30 to 33 percent representation of women to ensure a critical mass. Smaller numbers may

Box 4.7 Women Played an Active Political Role
in Post-Conflict East Timor

In East Timor, women were active in the liberation movement and the transition to independence. East Timorese women held 26 percent of the seats in the Constituent Assembly, which drafted the nation's new constitution in March 2002. The new constitution contains articles confirming equal rights for women and men. Moreover, women held three of the top cabinet positions—Minister of Justice, Minister of Finance, and Secretary of the Planning Commission.

East Timorese women's organizations played crucial political roles during and after independence. Upon independence in 1999, they immediately began lobbying for women's participation in nation building and the full integration of women's issues into the new constitution. Women's groups such as FOKUPER and the East-Timorese Women's Network pushed for initiatives to advance women's rights, such as the affirmative action campaign to establish a quota of 30 percent for female members of the Constituent Assembly (which became the national parliament upon independence). The quota was ultimately rejected, but women's representation in the Assembly ended up being very close to this target.

International organizations and women's rights' advocates also played a critical supporting role. For example, UNIFEM conducted workshops to train women to participate in elections for the Constituent Assembly, training nearly 145 participants in democratic principles of governance, women's rights, and leadership (Strickland and Duvvury 2003). In the end, 26 workshop participants registered as candidates for the 2001 Consultative Assembly election, which was 10 percent of female candidates; 24 women (26 percent) were elected to the Constituent Assembly (UNIFEM Web site).

lead to the "masculinization" of women rather than the "femininization" of politics—i.e., women adopting masculine attitudes and values prevailing in the political arena instead of changing them.

However, rules for quotas are not enough—it is implementation of the quotas that counts. Implementation can benefit from clear regulations, pressure from women's organizations, and sanctions for noncompliance [International Institute for Democracy and Electoral Assistance (IDEA) 2002]. One drawback of officially imposed quotas is that they can be considered essentially undemocratic—voluntary adoption of quotas by parties on their own party lists is preferable. Both cases require a strong commitment to gender balance.

• *Assessing impact.* There is a need to go beyond numbers in supporting gender balance in political participation (International IDEA 2002). It is important to assess the gender balance impact at the decisionmaking level in politics and its influence on society in general. Various indicators have been used, such as a growing consciousness of gender issues in society, the inclusion of gender issues in the political agenda, and legislative changes that are important for women (Hamadeh-Banerjee 2000). "The OSCE Handbook" refers to the proportion of men and women going to the polls, elected to public bodies, or appointed to public office (OSCE 2001; Strickland and Duvvury 2003). Experiences from Scandinavian countries also suggest various effects: reactions to female politicians may change as they acquire political legitimacy; the political culture will be less formal and less ceremonious as women are usually briefer and more to the point; and the nature of the political discourse may change as gender issues gradually become subject to serious political debate. Although it is difficult to establish causality, the effects of larger numbers of female politicians cannot be separated from what happens outside the political arena in society at large (Dahlerup 2001).

The list of policy options is not exhaustive, as the authors could not study the large specialized literature on elections, democracy, and power sharing (e.g., International IDEA 1997, 1998, 2002). More balanced gender participation in political processes will be hard to achieve if men continue to dominate the contents, culture, and rules of political institutions and decisionmaking processes. Women's increased participation in politics will only be truly valued when there is a shift in underlying gender power relations—a long-term effort that goes beyond the political domain.

CHAPTER 5

Gender, Informal Peace Processes, and Rebuilding Civil Society

Overview

INFORMAL PEACE PROCESSES ARE usually complementary to formal peace processes, but are not limited to them. The main *gender difference* is that more women than men tend to become active in informal processes. Informal peace activities often provide a springboard for women to enter public and political arenas and to become organized, often informally, but also by a more structured approach through CSOs.

An important *gender-role change* is that conflict offers many women the opportunity to enter informal peace processes. Women's engagement usually expands rapidly during conflict and tends to continue after conflict. While women focus initially on issues directly related to conflict and peace, gradually they start to cover broader issues. Many individual women and women's CSOs in conflict have assumed the roles and tasks of public institutions, undertaken all forms of relief work, channeled international assistance to recipients, lobbied to incorporate rights and specific provisions in peace accords, and encouraged women to participate in elections. The *key development challenge* is to support these women and women's CSOs (also men and men's CSOs), not only during but also after conflict, as they can form the foundation for a strong and more inclusive civil and political society after conflict, which is essential to effective, sustainable, and more inclusive reconstruction and development efforts.

Policy options include: strengthening the capacity of individual women and women's CSOs to bridge the gap between informal and formal peace processes; encouraging and training men and women in informal peace processes to make the shift toward formal processes; and involving individual women and women's CSOs actively in post-conflict rehabilitation and reconstruction. Community-driven reconstruction approaches can provide a unique opportunity to engage local women and men in jump-starting the local reconstruction process and helping to bridge the divide between crisis and development. International agencies can also assist in restructuring, professionalizing, and providing longer-term support to women's CSOs.

Support for these organizations during and after conflict can strengthen the foundations of post-conflict civil society, which can make a critical contribution to the implementation of peace accords and a wide range of rehabilitation and development activities.[35] The same applies to different forms of community-driven development efforts, which often emerge in less formalized settings in an attempt to meet urgent needs resulting from conflict. These organizational forms are also highly relevant in post-conflict reconstruction. As Bessell (2001) points out, in many conflict situations it is precisely the socially constructed gender roles that allow women a greater scope to become major advocates for peace and reconciliation.

Gender Roles in Informal Peace Processes

Women often identify informal peace processes as an opportunity to enter public and political arenas and to become organized, particularly in the nongovernmental sector. Moreover, women are often perceived as "not political," which enables them to access information and pressure authorities to provide services to minimize the impact of conflict on the civilian population (Strickland and Duvvury 2003, quoting Manchanda 2001). Also, women's limited access to formal peace talks and negotiations tends to encourage their participation in informal peace processes, as was the case in Colombia (see box 5.1). In Somalia,

---

Box 5.1 Women Rally to Promote Peace in Colombia

As Colombia's conflict expanded in the 1990s, women's civil society activism evolved from mainly humanitarian relief work to active peacemaking. They developed a complex network of national and local organizations that worked to gain a foothold in peace negotiations and, when the negotiations under President Pastrana collapsed, to develop a common civil society agenda for peace. Women at the community level directly mediated between the warring factions to avoid escalation, symbolically declaring their villages "peace communities" and liaising with armed actors to establish informal humanitarian agreements. However, this social activism came at a price—by 2002, 17 percent of assassinated or disappeared leaders and activists throughout Colombia were women (Rojas 2004).

women also became active at the local level to try to prevent their sons from being recruited by fighting forces or local warlords.[36]

Yet, informal peace processes are not the exclusive domain of women-run organizations. Men and men-led organizations are also involved in various ways. For example, churches played an active role in building political consensus and supporting national reconciliation in Angola, Liberia, and Sudan. Male journalists, human rights activists, and students actively participated in informal peace processes in Indonesia and Rwanda. However, these activities have not been looked at from a gender perspective and therefore do not increase our understanding of the different roles that women and men play. An exception is the Moser and McIlwaine (2001) study that examined whether female-dominated and male-dominated organizations played different roles in the peace processes in Colombia and Guatemala. The study found that there were often higher levels of trust in women-run than in men-run organizations, men sometimes played important roles within women-run organizations, and women were also integrated into male-dominated organizations. The authors noted that the higher trust placed in women-run organizations can play a central role in formulating and implementing strategies to reduce violence and efforts to rebuild social capital. Quoting Moser and McIlwaine, Corrin (2004) argues that recognizing the limitations of female-dominated organizations should not exaggerate their importance, but instead underlines the importance of gender analysis that emphasizes "female and male members both in formal organisations, as well as in informal networks of trust and reciprocity." Additional studies are needed to assess gender roles in informal peace processes.

Discussing women's involvement in peace in the decade-long Bougainville conflict that erupted in 1988, Bessell (2001) points out that the women's groups were not "allowed" a political space—they claimed it for themselves when they had no other means of returning normalcy to their lives. She draws two main lessons. First, both collectively and individually, women can contribute considerably to conflict management—often through imaginative and courageous approaches that men may not consider appropriate or deem acceptable in a society racked by open and armed conflict (see box 5.2). Second, despite the value of women's efforts during conflict, ongoing and deeply entrenched views about women's roles militate against them engaging in the political arena or formally entering decisionmaking processes. The paradox is evident—demonstrating the value of including women in conflict management is not necessarily enough to validate their claim to a more public voice. She notes that while the important and often powerful role of informal mechanisms should not

---

Box 5.2 Women's Peace Activism Brought on Pivotal
Changes in Sierra Leone

In May 2000, with the RUF (Revolutionary United Front) flouting the
1999 Lomé accords, a group of elderly women came together and de-
manded a meeting with Foday Sankoh. Arriving at the RUF compound,
they were mistreated and insulted. Frustrated, the women tried a different tactic. They collectively hitched up their skirts, bent over, and bared
themselves to Sankoh and his coterie. In Sierra Leone, such an action by
women is the worst curse that can be brought upon anyone. The news
had a galvanizing effect on the country. Sierra Leoneans felt they had an
obligation to uphold the women's honor and support the curse. But the
women's actions also gave people courage to stand up to the RUF.
Coinciding with the arrival of the new UN mission and British Special
Forces and coupled with subsequent demonstrations, the women's
protest was pivotal in the struggle for peace and culminated in Sankoh's
arrest (Mazurana and Carlson 2004).

---

be underestimated, nor should these mechanisms be undermined,
it does not follow that the existence and preservation of informal
mechanisms depends on the ongoing exclusion of women from formal
decisionmaking processes.

While much of the literature reviewed acknowledges the important
role that women can play in reconciliation and informal peace
processes, some observers caution that, when such work is seen as an
extension of women's "natural" role in society, it is taken for granted
and risks perpetuating gender inequality (S. Anderson 1999). When
this work is taken for granted, it goes unrecognized, is stripped of its
political meaning, and is rendered invisible. When does capitalizing on
women's strength in informal peace processes become tantamount to
perpetuating traditional gender stereotypes that rationalize inequality
and domination? Some critics argue that the values and attitudes that
give rise to these stereotypes are inextricably linked to the values and
attitudes that give rise to conflict itself. S. Anderson notes how the
Women in Black movement in Belgrade tried to address this dilemma
as they campaigned against the conflict in the former Yugoslavia.[37]

As discussed in chapter 9, below, in many development agencies,
including the World Bank, there is a growing emphasis on community-
driven development (CDD) approaches and their relevance and application in post-conflict reconstruction. With its focus on local-level
execution and participation, CDD has considerable potential to

encourage women's participation and to engender reconstruction and development processes. CDD provides excellent opportunities for women to take part or, more generally, to adopt a gender-specific approach in program design and implementation and in benefit distribution.

Dynamics: Readjusting the Work on Peace, Rehabilitation, and Development

Conflict offers windows of opportunity for CSO development, particularly for women's groups. In addition to their active engagement in informal peace processes (peace marches, reconciliation ceremonies, regional consultations, lobbying, and media campaigns), at times they have managed to enter formal peace processes or played important roles in propping up key institutions and services during conflict. In Burundi, Cambodia, Guatemala, Rwanda, and Yugoslavia, women's organizations worked to rebuild core institutions and services, often defining their efforts as "resisting conflict."[38] Women tried to keep alive the memory and idea of a "normal situation" (NUPI 2001) by becoming active in health centers, day-care facilities, summer camps for children, home schooling, and distributing food or clothes to the elderly (Kumar 2000).

Organizations also adapt after conflict. Relief and development agencies have encouraged the establishment of women's organizations to channel international assistance to beneficiaries, often women (Walsh 1997; Kumar 2000). Women's organizations have also tried, not always successfully, to ensure the enforcement of legal rights and provisions embodied in peace accords [UN Center for Human Settlements (UNCHS) 1999]. Furthermore, various women's organizations have been involved in a variety of post-conflict rehabilitation activities, ranging from relief work and the distribution of material and financial resources, to the protection of human rights and design of development projects. As a result, many women's organizations have been able to redirect their efforts toward newly emerging needs and opportunities during and after conflict. In Georgia, most women's organizations had a history of charity work, but gradually refocused on encouraging women to take part in parliamentary elections, participate in local governance, and promote self-reliance (Morton et al. 2001). On a less positive note, many CSOs, especially women's organizations, have difficulty surviving after a conflict ends (see box 5.3), which suggests the need for continued external support (El-Bushra 2003).

Box 5.3 Women's Refugee NGOs Lose Power
in Post-Conflict Guatemala

With assistance from NGOs and UNHCR, Guatemalan refugee women organized themselves in Mexico and became active in refugee communities. They supported incorporating women into community life by promoting training in literacy, human rights, reproductive health, and leadership skills. They later devoted most of their efforts to repatriating refugees and were among the representatives of refugee communities in negotiations with government officials on land rights, rights for returnees, and other issues. In these negotiations, they secured women's rights to be co-owners of land allocated to returning families (normally ceded to male household heads).

When the refugee women who had so enthusiastically participated in these organizations returned home to Guatemala, the space for female social and political organization was drastically diminished for a number of reasons. First, women and men returned to rural communities that were much poorer than the refugee camps, so the women had little space to make use of their newly acquired skills and experience. Second, the returnees were widely dispersed, so they often felt isolated in their new communities and separated from those with whom they had developed relations of trust. Third, they missed the support of NGOs, international organizations, and their own organizations, which had mobilized, supported, and guided them in exile. Fourth, they encountered renewed hostility from male family members due to their continued community organization and participation. The men no longer looked favorably on their wives or daughters engaging in activities outside the home. In various cases, the male leadership even ignored the legal principle of co-ownership affirmed in Mexico, and sometimes threatened women who tried to insist on their land rights. Under these circumstances, women's organizations established in the refugee camps continued to operate, but did not survive well. The development agencies working in the returnee areas were not quite able to harness the potential contributions that returnee women could make.[39]

Development Challenges: The Need for Sustained External Support

The increasing involvement of women and women's organizations in informal peace processes or relief work during conflict may form an important breeding ground and bridge into formal peace and political processes and thus contribute to a more vibrant and inclusive post-conflict civil society. To reach these goals, a conscious policy should be put in place, as initial gains are easily lost in a post-conflict setting. The Guatemalan refugee case described above shows the need for sustained external support. Agencies working in refugee camps should try to ensure longer-term support for female empowerment after refugees have returned home. A UNHCR (2001) evaluation found that greater collaboration on gender issues during the return process between UN agencies and implementing partners and follow-up training on gender issues in returnee communities might have helped to mitigate the negative impacts on women. In addition, strengthening women's groups and organizations outside the context of refugee camps requires improving women's access to labor-saving devices and a better distribution of the family workload. The will to participate is not enough if the women do not also have the time to devote to organizing and engaging in community activities. Finally, to sustain women's gains during conflict, men in general and husbands/partners, in particular, must learn to accept the reality that migration, economic decline, and war constitute an irreversible set of experiences that permanently change women's lives. At the same time, WSP finds that the politicized context of post-conflict societies leaves few neutral and impartial spaces for dialogue. Postwar political systems are often barely developed and provide few institutionalized mechanisms for discussion and communication. The authoritarian tendencies of many postwar governments are also not conducive to open communication, and participation is often sacrificed in the name of speed (WSP Web site).

Policy Options

Support Women's Organizations/CSOs to Bridge the Gap between Informal and Formal Peace Processes

Informal peace processes can be a fertile breeding ground for women to enter the political arena during and after conflict. Women's peace efforts in particular have received increasing international attention, although some agencies remain reluctant to support these activities, perhaps due to their underappreciation of informal peace processes relative to formal peace initiatives. However, a key lesson is that the two processes are closely interrelated and cannot be separated. The energy and activism that many women's organizations exhibit in informal peace processes can be harnessed to enhance their contribution to formal peace processes [Organisation for Economic Co-operation and

Development/Development Assistance Committee (OECD/DAC) 1998; UN 2002; GTZ 2001]. Policy options include:

- *Capacity building and training of women's organizations.* This could help the organizations to better understand and operate in peace processes. Training topics include conflict resolution and negotiation techniques, the mechanisms of peace processes, lobbying, information dissemination, and language.
- *Increasing the visibility and exposure of women's organizations.* Many informal peace initiatives go unnoticed. Women's organizations require support to gain attention from society in general and from participants in formal peace processes in particular. Support would be important to set up or strengthen networks of women's organizations and gender platforms to advocate gender equality, exchange information and experiences, and mobilize women. Examples of such networks are *Femmes Africa Solidarité* (Geneva), the Mano River Women's Peace Network (based in Guinea but covering also Liberia and Sierra Leone), the Women in Black Peace Network (Belgrade, former Yugoslavia), and International Alert's Women Building Peace Campaign (United Kingdom, but the campaign was international).
- *Encourage links between women's organizations and formal peace processes.* External support can facilitate contacts between women's organizations and actors in the formal peace process (see box 5.4) or, in turn, encourage formal peace participants to involve women's organizations.
- *Support female civil society leaders to become formal political actors.* In various post-conflict countries, female civil society leaders have used the opportunity to become civil servants or politicians (see box 5.4), despite some reluctance to enter formal politics.[40]

Care should be taken not to reinforce the stereotype that women are only active in informal processes and men in formal processes—the opposite should be supported. The participation of male or mixed organizations in informal peace processes and female politicians or activists in formal peace processes should be encouraged.

Informal Peace Processes as the Breeding Ground for Formal Peace Processes

Informal peace processes can be a fertile breeding ground for women and men to enter the post-conflict political arena. In some cases, female civil society leaders may be reluctant to enter formal politics, for

---

Box 5.4 Rwandan Women Move from Informal
        to Formal Politics

Anecdotal evidence from Rwanda shows that many women elected to
local women's councils in 1998 had previous experience as leaders or
members of women's or mixed organizations. In 1998, the government
began a process to elect women's councils at the local level. The 10-person
councils, each elected at the township (*cellule* and *sector*), county
(*commune*), and prefecture levels, provided an opportunity for local
women to have a say in issues that affect their communities, such as
health, education, and development. They also manage the women's
communal funds and serve as local representatives of the Ministry of
Gender and Women in Development. At the township level, the councils
exclusively consist of women. At the sector and prefecture levels,
women gained about one-half of the seats (4 of the 10 seats are reserved
for women). Women's grassroots activism and government and donor
encouragement for women's organizations opened up this political
space for women to participate in public arenas (Newbury and Baldwin
2001). Women now face the challenge of finding time to participate
in these committees and ensure that their issues are not marginalized
in political structures and relegated to committees instead of central
decisionmaking processes (WCWRC 2001).

---

example, stating that political parties are not sensitive to their needs
and that their organizations can be more effective if they remain politically independent. This was the case in Georgia, where very few leaders of women's organizations attempted to jump from civil society into
the political arena (Morton et al. 2001).

Women's Organizations and Other CSOs as the Foundation for Post-Conflict Civil Society

Efforts to strengthen civil society during and after conflict should pay
particular attention to women's organizations. They form an essential
part of civil society (El-Bushra 2003) and have the potential to promote women's leadership, to build awareness of women's rights, and
to contribute to gender equality. They can be instrumental in implementing and monitoring peace accords and channeling humanitarian
and development assistance to targeted populations (e.g., Byrne 1996;
Kumar 2001). However, a USAID study (2001) that looked at
women's organizations in a number of post-conflict settings found that
their impact was limited because of a lack of communication and

cooperation among the organizations. As a result, efforts were often duplicated, the image of women's organizations in the public mind was undermined, and skills and expertise were not shared across organizations. Some considerations in channeling support to women's organizations include:

- *Long-term support to women's organizations.* In all conflict phases, support is needed for the formation and strengthening of women's organizations, the articulation of gender agendas, and to promote women candidates for public and political office. UNHCR was instrumental in forming many volunteer women's groups during the conflict in Bosnia and Herzegovina; many of the groups established themselves as full-fledged women's organizations after the conflict (Kumar 2001). However, a long-term commitment from agencies, particularly financial, is required to make women's organizations sustainable. In countries such as Bosnia and Herzegovina, Cambodia, El Salvador, Georgia, Guatemala, and Rwanda, most women's organizations largely, if not exclusively, depended on international assistance during and after conflict (Kumar 2000). The continuation of international support to these organizations is particularly crucial when the conflict is over, when international funding and humanitarian assistance levels decline rapidly, and when developing agencies may be reluctant to follow up the work of humanitarian agencies. USAID (2001) notes that in an environment of shifting donor priorities, the short duration of assistance programs prevented recipient organizations from developing their own priorities—lacking their own funds, many organizations had to abandon their original plans and struggle to establish new programs in areas where they had little expertise. External support should consider longer-term funding, funding a portion of core costs in addition to program costs, and helping organizations to improve fund-raising skills (Kumar 2001).
- *Promote development of women's CSOs.* To ensure sustainability, women's organizations can be assisted to change mandates, goals, and activities and to explore possibilities for income-generating activities. This can include training in management, leadership, lobbying, and advocacy. These activities can increase their professionalism, thereby raising the organization's status among male counterparts (Kumar 2000, 2001; OSCE 2001).
- *Integrate women's organizations in longer-term development and rehabilitation efforts.* Support for women's organizations needs to become a more integral part of efforts to rehabilitate post-conflict societies. Agencies can seek to contract women's organizations in

development assistance programs related to health, income generation, social work, democracy, and human rights advocacy and in implementing peace accords. It is important to note that these organizations not only support women—they can and very often do participate in development programs that provide benefits to the community as a whole.

- *Improve donor coordination within a longer-term gender strategy.* USAID (2001) notes that there has been little or no donor coordination in supporting women's post-conflict organizations. Donor agencies have tended to work independently without adequate information and understanding of one another's programs. International assistance to women's organizations also suffered because the development community lacked a coherent policy and strategic framework for assisting and promoting gender equality in post-conflict societies. Such a framework may not only provide an overall rationale for policy and program coherence, but also can promote more meaningful donor coordination and avoid duplication (Kumar 2001).

Three additional points are worth noting:

1. Timing is crucial in supporting women's organizations. The right moment for support aimed at sustainability must come during wartime (Meintjes et al. 2001) or between the end of a conflict and the beginning of the reconstruction process (Sörensen 1998; UNDP 2003). Organizations of refugee women, female combatants, and others will begin to disintegrate as members return to a normal life. Therefore, it is important to integrate them into existing organizations at their new places of residence or to organize new social structures in receiving communities.
2. Greater attention is likely warranted on supporting grassroots and networks of women organizations rather than focusing solely on large and well-established women's organizations. The latter are often led by well-connected women, who may be acting more in the interests of ruling elites or political dynasties— USAID (2001) found that well-established and connected women's organizations tended to receive the lion's share of international assistance.
3. On a related note, an exclusive focus on CSOs may not be helpful to address gender balance. A recent trend is to integrate relevant actors, including CSOs, in more encompassing public-private partnerships or networks, but these efforts have not been gender evaluated.

CHAPTER 6

Gender-Sensitizing the Post-Conflict Legal Framework

Overview

CONFLICT IS GENERALLY ASSOCIATED with a failure of governance and a breakdown of the rule of law, which may be at the root of the conflict or a result of the conflict. The post-conflict transition period often provides an opportunity to rebuild society, not only in physical but also in legislative and institutional terms. Conflict societies often have an opportunity to undergo a transformation in the security, political, and socioeconomic realms that is usually accompanied by constitutional and legal reforms. In most cases the aim is not to re-create the pre-conflict situation, but rather to introduce reforms and address the factors and conditions that may have given rise to or exacerbated the conflict in the first place. In the political realm, most post-conflict transitions involve the adoption of more democratic, accountable, and inclusive forms of government.

In this chapter, two key issues are highlighted. The first is the post-conflict momentum to rewrite and gender-sensitize the constitution and other laws. The second is the challenge to ensure justice and accountability by providing adequate judicial recourse for the (sexual) crimes committed against women and men and by guaranteeing women's and men's equal access to appropriate legal support services.

From a *gender perspective,* the legal reforms are the moment to enshrine gender-equality issues (such as women's and men's equal access to land, property, education, work, and politics) and other basic human rights in the constitution and to formalize women's and men's democratic representation and participation in all decision-making structures of the government and society at large. Furthermore, the transition period provides the momentum to restore justice and accountability mechanisms and to reestablish the rule of law. In this context, judicial mechanisms need to pay more attention to *gender-specific issues.* For example, women's specific needs must be

77

considered in formulating reparations and rehabilitation policies. Women and men should receive similar compensation for similar human rights violations committed against them. Difficult GBV issues, such as rape and other forms of sexual violence, must be treated with the utmost sensitivity in court sessions. Whereas some international tribunals have been successful, there is no information on gender aspects of local judicial mechanisms, such as the Gacaca ("on the grass") courts in Rwanda.

Some post-conflict societies tend to revert to particularly gender-insensitive, traditional law. *Key challenges* are to extend gender equality provisions to nonstatutory and customary law and to develop effective implementation mechanisms. A final challenge is to develop judicial mechanisms that do not marginalize women's experiences and do not consider women only as victims but also as perpetrators of violence in conflict settings.

Supporting governments—through awareness-raising and information campaigns—to ratify, respect, and implement relevant international standards would be a first *policy option* to ensure women's and men's rights in conflict situations. A second option would be to develop and enforce gender-sensitive legislation at the national level, for example, by involving women and men in drafting new legislation. Other options are to inform and train women and men on their rights and to encourage the judiciary to enforce gender-sensitive laws.

With regard to judicial mechanisms, a primary *policy option* is to encourage them to acknowledge, condemn, and prosecute all crimes committed *by* women and men *against* women and men in conflict situations. The judiciary could help courts assist survivors and witnesses to share their experiences. Facilities could include establishing a reporting system, protecting survivors and witnesses, sensitizing staff to deal with GBV survivors, and developing a more equal system to recruit female and male staff. Finally, agencies could encourage courts to provide female and male survivors with similar reimbursement of expenses, provision of services, and restoration of rights.

Gender-Specific Laws, Adequate Judicial Recourse, and Equal Access to Legal Services

Gender-Specific Legal Provisions

There is limited literature on gender-sensitizing legal reform processes in post-conflict societies. The existing literature recognizes that the post-conflict phase provides an opportunity to gender-sensitize and update laws, but it shows less clearly whether there are crucial differences between conflict and nonconflict situations. In both situations, it is difficult to design and enforce laws that are gender-sensitive and culturally appropriate. However, to the extent that laws are adapted to the local culture and the more that general awareness is raised on gender equality and women's issues, the greater the chance that gendered legal reforms will be adopted and implemented.

Nonetheless, to be effective, gender equality and other basic human rights need to be enshrined in the country's legal framework. This includes ensuring that women's and men's participation in decision-making structures of the government and society is guaranteed formally, as is often the case, and in practice, which often is not. Many laws still include provisions that discriminate against women or place them at a disadvantage, especially regarding access to land and property. Evaluation of legal reforms should include an examination of all laws and regulations with a gender lens (NUPI 2001). In many cases, legal frameworks have not been updated and often have been inherited from the colonial period. In Sierra Leone, Richards et al. (2004) point out that laws governing rape date back to the British 1861 Offences Against Persons Act, and because most provisions have not been updated, the protection the laws afford women is often only marginally better than what is provided under customary and Islamic law. For example, under the latter two (which govern about 65 percent of the population), girls are considered marriageable once breasts have developed and menses started (which can be as early as 11 or 12 years old), and a married woman is considered a minor whose husband has the right to prosecute or defend on her behalf.

Adequate Judicial Recourse and Access to Legal Services for Women and Men

Most policy discussions on gender, justice, and accountability focus on institutional structures, arrangements, and procedures to guarantee effective access to legal support services for women, as well as judicial recourse for crimes committed during conflict, especially those against women (e.g., OECD/DAC 1998). However, accountability must go beyond punishing perpetrators and instead focus on establishing the rule of law and a just social and political order. Ensuring justice and accountability can be undertaken at the local, national, and international levels, through a variety of judicial mechanisms. These include: the International Criminal Court (ICC); ad hoc tribunals such as the International Criminal Tribunals for Former Yugoslavia (ICTY) and Rwanda (ICTR); special courts and tribunals such as the Special Court for Sierra Leone; and national justice systems. Nonjudicial methods such as truth and reconciliation commissions, and traditional mechanisms such as Gacaca courts in Rwanda, can also play an important role (Rehn and Sirleaf 2002).

Judicial mechanisms are not always able to provide equal access to justice for women and men. The literature highlights issues such as insufficient consideration of women's needs and interests in the formulation of reparations and rehabilitation policies, unequal compensation of women and men for similar human rights violations, and insensitivity in treating difficult issues such as GBV during court sessions (Goldblatt and Meintjes 1998). ICTY and, to a lesser degree, ICTR may be exceptions; these tribunals have attempted to provide justice for conflict survivors, prosecute crimes committed during conflict, and provide judicial recourse. They have addressed GBV issues against women and men in conflict situations and have offered protection, medical and psychological support, and logistics assistance to female and male survivors and witnesses. They have also established special structures and procedures to work with female and male survivors and provided specialized staff training (Bouta and Frerks 2002).

Dynamics: Nonstatutory Law and the Legacy of Violence

A particular dynamic in sensitizing the post-conflict legal framework is that customary law may sideline statutory law. In many cases, traditional norms have a greater impact on women's positions than formal norms in constitutions or statutes. Even if reasonably progressive constitutions and legal codes are adopted (see box 6.1), enforcement remains a challenge. In Sierra Leone, Richards et al. (2004) point out that local custom often conflicts with national law; areas where custom and legal rights diverge include depriving widows of property or allowing the seizure of a widow's property by the dead husband's lineage, "women damage" (adultery), induction of minors into closed associations (without informed consent), and denying education to pregnant school girls.

The other dynamic for most post-conflict societies lies in handling the legacy of violence, especially in finding a balance between prosecution versus reconciliation and accountability versus impunity. Solving these dilemmas requires tailor-made approaches that take into account not only the conflict's history, but also the society's cultural and social values. Several courts have been established to manage conflict-related

Box 6.1 Taking Constitutional Steps in Post-Conflict
Afghanistan

The Afghanistan Judicial Reform Commission has the task of reviewing domestic laws for consistency with treaty obligations, such as the Convention on the Elimination of All Forms of Discrimination against Women (CEDAW), which was signed on March 5, 2003, and to incorporate its norms into all existing and new penal and civil codes. At the same time, the Bonn Agreement provided for a Constitutional Commission to prepare a draft document for consideration by a Constitutional *Loya Jirga* to begin prior to 2004. At the time of writing there continued to be tensions between international norms, the more modernizing elements within the *Loya Jirga* and the government, and more traditional elements of Afghan society (International Crisis Group (ICG) 2003).

atrocities in Europe and Sub-Saharan Africa, but no gender analysis of these processes appears to be available.

Development Challenges: Post-Conflict Legal Foundations and Engendering the Rule of Law

As part of a broader post-conflict rehabilitation process, many countries revise the constitution and laws to reflect new political realities, changes in power relations, ideological objectives, and compliance with international norms (adapted from Sörensen 1998). It is here that the foundations for postconflict society are laid and where there can be an opportunity and momentum to gender-sensitize the legal framework. Constitutions determine people's economic and social rights and can play a central role in empowerment. Particularly in countries where customary law, social norms, and social practices restrict women's roles, constitutional protection of women's rights can have a longer-term impact in promoting greater equality and equity (Sheckler 2002). Although many gender issues in legal frameworks are also prevalent in nonconflict societies and very hard to address, these issues are exacerbated by conflict. However, post-conflict reconstruction generally offers an opportunity for more comprehensive reforms.

In the end, legal reforms are only as effective as their implementation. Some authors argue that CEDAW and other such conventions have limited utility or impact in some conflict-affected countries, such as Afghanistan and Algeria, because ratifying and implementing them

Box 6.2 Centers Provide Legal Advice to Women
              in Southeastern Europe

In Bosnia and Herzegovina, seven local legal experts established the
Center of Legal Assistance to Women in 1997. The center initially provided information to women on property, housing, and labor rights,
and it gradually started helping clients to realize their legal rights.
Because of its success, its number of clients and cooperation with similar centers elsewhere in the former Yugoslavia increased rapidly. In
2001, the center started training on women's rights and lobbying for
changes in laws (Kvinna till Kvinna 2000).

As part of postwar peace-building and conflict prevention efforts, the
Stability Pact for Southeastern Europe (SP) GTF assisted countries to
ratify international agreements such as CEDAW and to establish governmental commissions and institutions working for gender equality.
These institutions collected gender-disaggregated statistics, lobbied for
electoral reform, and reviewed legislation from a gender perspective.
According to GTF, good practices from the region include agreements
on quotas for female candidates on the lists of political parties in
Macedonia, Montenegro, and Serbia and the establishment of different
gender equality governmental mechanisms or parliamentary bodies in
Bosnia and Herzegovina, Croatia, Montenegro, and Vojvodina (SP GTF
2002).

is voluntary (e.g., Farr 2002). However, implementation prospects
may improve if ratification also includes education and sensitization
campaigns that explain and promote women's and men's equal legal
rights and legal assistance (see box 6.2). Culturally appropriate justifi-
cations for reform need to be developed to mobilize broad support
(ICG 2003).

Providing justice and accountability can be a first step toward re-
establishing the rule of law in post-conflict societies, but the major
challenge is to gender-sensitize the rule of law. Judicial mechanisms
have often tended to marginalize and overlook women's experiences,
perhaps because they require addressing issues that do not affect men
to the same extent (i.e., sexual violence), the fact that women find it
difficult to testify (which is often exacerbated by lack of personal security), or that commissioners, government, or the general public are
reluctant to acknowledge women's war experiences (Pankhurst 2000).
In Sierra Leone, although legal structures were reestablished almost
everywhere in the country, only a small number of women, primarily
in the western area, and those with sufficient funds can access the formal legal system (Richards et al. 2004). In addition, the tendency to

perceive women only as victims must be reconsidered—although this may be less obvious, a balanced approach must consider that women too can be perpetrators of violence and crimes.

Policy Options

Increase Commitment to Existing International Standards

The problem is not so much the absence of relevant international standards, but the lack of implementation and respect for them (ICRC 2003). A first step to ensure women's and men's rights in conflict situations may be the ratification of existing international standards, such as CEDAW (see box 6.3), the International Humanitarian Law (IHL), and the

---

Box 6.3 CEDAW Gender Balances Uganda's Constitution

CEDAW served as a starting point for rewriting Uganda's constitution in 1995. The government held national consultations to prepare for drafting the new constitution. Women's NGOs felt strongly that this process was not designed to include women in a significant way and started their own parallel consultation process. They also mobilized to get women elected to the Constituent Assembly, which would draft the constitution. Once the Constituent Assembly was established, its female members formed a women's caucus to develop a united position on the proposals that would come before the assembly. The women working on proposals for the new constitution referred to CEDAW as establishing a minimum acceptable standard, and the convention is reflected in a number of provisions in Uganda's constitution. Its first provision, which declares the constitution's guiding principles, states that the need for gender balance and fair representation is to inform the implementation of the constitution and all government policies and programs. The Ugandan Constitution's Bill of Rights states that rights are to be enjoyed without discrimination on the basis of sex. The constitution also contains strong guarantees on women's political participation based on CEDAW's conceptualization of equality, which recognizes the need for temporary special measures to speed the achievement of equality and stipulates that these measures are not discriminatory (Article 4). The constitution reserves a number of parliamentary seats for women. It requires that each administrative district have at least one female representative and at least one-third of the seats in local government (city, municipal, and district councils) be filled by women (UNIFEM 1998; Mukiibi 2000).

Convention for the Suppression of the Traffic in Persons and of the Exploitation of the Prostitution of Others.[41] Implementation of these standards is usually a slow process, and awareness is often lacking among government officials, legal specialists, and security actors such as the army and police, but also the population at large. To raise awareness, the ICRC has tried to promote the IHL widely, for example, by disseminating information about the IHL's essential concepts to women's organizations, their families, and communities in Sierra Leone and Somalia (ICRC 2003).[42] Richards et al. (2004) suggest that since Sierra Leone is signatory to many human rights conventions, which are incorporated into national law, local lawyers working in collaboration with rural development agencies or women's organizations could appeal actions under customary law that contradict national law in class action lawsuits.

Gender-Sensitize the Legal Framework

Whereas the application of international regulations may improve the protection of women's and men's rights, they can also be drawn upon to reform and gender-sensitize national and customary laws. Options include:

- *Ensure the involvement of women and men in drafting new legislation.* It is not always easy for women and men to participate in legal reforms after conflict. For example, women's organizations in Bosnia and Herzegovina were not involved in drafting new laws (Kvinna till Kvinna 2000), but were more successful in Cambodia and Eritrea (see box 6.4).
- *Inform and train women and men on their legal rights.* Disseminating information on new laws is important [Swedish International Development Agency (SIDA) 2000]. For example, translating legal documents into local languages may ensure that women and men of different ethnic groups are aware of their rights. Moreover, legal literacy programs for women and men should accompany legislative changes and the establishment of institutions that provide legal education and counseling to women and men (Byrne 1996; UN 2002). Training can focus on making women and men aware of their rights, which may increase the chances that human rights violations are reported and legal mechanisms enforced (Turshen 2001).
- *Encourage the judiciary to enforce gender-sensitive laws.* Since the judiciary is a crucial player in the interpretation and enforcement of laws, judges and legal personnel should be sensitized on women's and men's human rights; this may raise their awareness and capacity to address gender issues.

Box 6.4 Inclusive Legislation Is Drafted in Cambodia
and Eritrea

In Cambodia, a consultative process that included women of all socioeconomic classes and from across the country accompanied the drafting
of the constitution during the UNCTAC (United Nations Transitional
Authority in Cambodia) period. As a result, the Cambodian Constitution grants women and men equal rights (Byrne 1996; UN 2002).

The Eritrean government led a broad public discussion in preparation
for its new constitution. Special commissions with male and female
members visited all regions to discuss the draft constitution. The new
constitution was ratified in 1997; it not only recognizes women's basic
human rights, but also grants women the right of access to land. The
constitution also prohibits female circumcision and makes dowry and
"bride price" illegal, while extending rights to maternity leave (Sörensen
1998). On the other hand, it does not include affirmative action clauses
to ensure female representation in high-level, decision-making positions,
as the National Union of Eritrean Women had proposed (Hale 2001).

Provide for the Establishment of a National Machinery for Gender Equality

Ideally, gender-sensitive legal frameworks should provide mechanisms
and structural frameworks that explicitly incorporate gender issues.
These can include ministries for women's affairs or gender and development, departments of women's affairs, offices on the status of
women, gender desks or focal points in line ministries, parliaments,
commissions on inequality, and ombudsman offices.

Encourage Judicial Mechanisms to Acknowledge, Condemn, and Prosecute All Crimes against Women and Men in Conflict Situations

Particularly at the international level, judicial mechanisms such as
the ICC and the two ad hoc tribunals increasingly pay attention to
women's and men's experiences in conflict situations. For example, the
tribunals have charged and found individuals guilty of committing
gender-based and sexual crimes, which has contributed to an emerging
jurisprudence (UN 2002; Rehn and Sirleaf 2002; Bouta and Frerks
2002). Some of these practices have also been applied at the national
level, for example, in truth and reconciliation commissions. Additional support could be considered for government institutions to

increase their compatibility with international regulations such as the Statute of the Criminal Court and thus to increase the number of successful domestic prosecutions (e.g., Kritz 1997).

Regarding GBV, the challenge lies at the national and local levels, where legal interventions are still needed on GBV prevention, protection of survivors, and prosecution of perpetrators. As case studies show [e.g., Democratic Republic of Congo[43] (DRC)], tackling the GBV issue in situations of ongoing violence and impunity is often extremely difficult and can best be combined with comprehensive efforts to restore the rule of law and to provide judicial protection and resources to survivors in general. Experience suggests that legal assistance remains vital, especially to:[44]

- Ensure the protection of women and men against GBV through existing laws or new legislation;
- Criminalize all forms of GBV—survivors must be protected from prosecution and perpetrators penalized;
- Pursue punishment proportionate to the crime, no matter where it was committed (a public or private venue), who committed it (a stranger or a "loved one"), and why it was committed (war, theft, or family or community control of members); and
- Provide survivors with legal means and assistance in the course of any criminal, civil, or other action against GBV perpetrators— e.g., enable them to claim and receive compensation.

Facilitate the Process for Victims and Witnesses to Share and Report Experiences

Other lessons to adequately address (sexual) crimes committed against women and men in conflict include the following:

- Establishing an *effective reporting and monitoring* system on human rights violations during conflict is crucial, especially to increase the chances of judicial recourse after conflict.
- Ensuring *support and protection of victims, their families, and witnesses before, during, and after the trials* (OSCE 2001; UN 2002). It is important to take into account potential traumas and possible differences in needs between women and men. For example, the ad hoc tribunals have established special victim and witness units, which arrange transport, provide psychological counseling, fund childcare facilities, handle attendance allowances, and help at-risk victims and witnesses to relocate. Their support usually stops after the trials. It is important, however, that women and men receive assistance either from the

judicial mechanisms or from other bodies such as NGOs to return home and to reintegrate.

- *Sensitizing legal staff in dealing with (GBV) crimes.* The ad hoc tribunals have trained investigators, prosecutors, judges, and protection and support officers to ensure victim and witness privacy and dignity.
- Considering *greater gender balance in staff.* Particularly, but not exclusively, in dealing with gender-based and sexual crimes, there is often a need for equivalence in sex between the victim and the investigator, the prosecutor, the protection and support officer, and even the judge.

Although the discussion of justice and accountability has focused on GBV crimes, judicial mechanisms and recourse should address gender issues broadly—e.g., women's and men's access and ownership of houses, land, and other assets (Pankhurst 2000; Women Building Peace 2001). Moreover, most lessons and best practices are derived from international judicial bodies and conventions. Agencies should consider how to raise the issue of gender, justice, and accountability in their dialogue with governments, especially when supporting judicial modernization programs in post-conflict countries.

CHAPTER 7

Gender and Work: Creating Equal Labor Market Opportunities

WOMEN'S PAID AND UNPAID WORK GENERALLY weighs more heavily in wartime.[45] While women's domestic burden increases during conflict, their opportunity to engage in paid work outside the household rises as well. Although women's growing responsibilities inside and outside the household are acknowledged and where relevant are referred to, the chapter is written from the latter point of view. It analyzes women's and men's different roles and positions with regard to agricultural work and informal and formal urban employment.

Overview

The domain of gender and work covers the relationship between gender and agricultural work and informal work and formal urban work. Regarding *gender-specific differences and gender role changes* in relation to work during conflict, many women take on tasks that their husbands or other male relatives had done previously. The women often become the new household head and the main breadwinner. At the same time, displacement and post-conflict unemployment undermine men's sense of identity as provider, which, in turn, often translates into anti-social behavior and violence directed at women. In the *agricultural sector,* women may take over responsibility for working the land, caring for livestock, trading, or carrying out wage labor outside the home. The key problem is that women are often denied access to, owning, and inheriting productive resources in their own names. This restricts the survival possibilities of female-headed households and widows, but also of women in general. In the post-conflict phase in particular—when prevailing labor divisions are reintroduced, land is scarce, and there are many claims on land, by residents and returnees—many women are rendered homeless and landless. In urban areas, a kind of "feminization" of the *informal sector* takes place during conflict. Women enter this sector more easily than the formal sector because it requires less education, training, and start-up capital, and they often continue to work in the sector after conflict. Women may regard work in the informal sector as a way of liberation and empowerment or as a means of exploitation and survival. Regarding the *formal sector,* key gender differences relate to unequal promotion opportunities, remuneration, rights, and so on for women and men. A limited number of women are formally employed compared to men. During conflict, however, formal employment opportunities for women are likely to increase, among other things, because of emerging war-related industries and the "economies of violence." Yet, the net effect during or after conflict is not clear as, for instance, the closure of large-scale enterprises and the collapse of government structures may well offset the increase in war-related jobs. In a number of cases, the influx of male returnees, including numerous male ex-soldiers and their prioritized employment, meant that women working in the formal sector were generally the first to lose their jobs, regardless of their position. In other cases, women who were encouraged to take up formal employment during conflict may have been able to retain higher labor force participation after conflict.

The major *development challenge* is to take advantage of and assist in sustaining positive gender role changes regarding work as a result of conflict. This would involve the design of economic assistance programs that build on women's and men's newly acquired skills, and encourage women and men to continue in their new tasks and activities.

One important contribution would be to try to reduce women's domestic and reproductive burdens, so that women who want to earn a living outside the home can do so. This should go hand in hand with efforts to reform gender-biased labor laws and raise awareness on gender equality issues in the workplace. Over the short term, agricultural policies need to restore women's and men's means of production, but over the longer term, they need to focus on ensuring more equal access to land and productive resources. In relation to informal urban employment, microcredit schemes have brought many women much-needed relief, but the schemes' economic sustainability and empowerment potential are often limited and should be complemented by other forms of support. Vocational training programs can be useful, but they must be based on sound market research and gender analysis. They should be adapted to women's and men's different skills and needs, but also avoid trapping women in traditional areas with limited market potential. The education, health, and civil service sectors—formal employment sectors that traditionally employ women—can be an important source of employment, but women can also be supported to apply new skills and experience gained during conflict. Options include issuing diplomas and certificates to formalize their qualifications and positive actions (such as hiring quotas and recruitment strategies) to employing more women in rehabilitation and development activities. Greater labor equality (e.g., pay, maternal leave, promotions) can also help over the long run.

Linking Gender and Work

Most of the literature on gender and work in conflict settings tends to focus on women's access to employment and income. There is little discussion or policy recommendations on the particular problems faced by young and adult males when, due to displacement or a lack of post-conflict employment opportunities, they are unable to access employment or stable income sources. While it is clear that the burden of displacement and conflict tends to fall disproportionately on women, the displacement and unemployment caused by conflict can also represent a radical dislocation for men and their sense of identity. Above all, male identity in most societies is to be the provider (breadwinner), to be responsible, and to provide financially for one's family. Unemployment undermines a key foundation of male identity and male perceptions of self-worth. In conflict-affected countries, however, unemployment can be substantially higher due to displacement and slow economic recovery after conflict. This erosion in male identity can be exacerbated when there is a sense that men have somehow failed as providers by "losing the war" or in some way have been powerless to prevent the displacement from taking place (adapted from Holtzman and Nezam 2004). When male identity and social roles are undermined, men tend to assert their masculinity through violence, alcohol or drug abuse, and other negative behaviors (Correia 2003). For unemployed and out of school young men, (re)joining the fighting forces can offer the status, identity, sense of belonging, and remuneration that are unavailable in a displacement camp or a devastated and economically weak post-conflict country (Barker 2003). In most societies, violence and other male antisocial behavior have a clear gender dimension, often adversely impacting women through sexual and reproductive health, and domestic and social violence directed at women and young girls (Barker 2002). In the end, creating meaningful post-conflict employment for men and women is key, but there has been little research on approaches that can encourage alternative versions of male identity and thus reduce negative gender impacts as countries transition out of conflict.

Regarding agricultural work, conflict tends to break down the prevailing labor division between women and men and forces women to take over tasks that men had done previously. Women often become household heads and the main breadwinners in the absence of their husbands or male relatives. They must earn a living, work the land, care for livestock, and trade or engage in paid labor outside the home. In some cases this may have been happening already as men moved to urban areas in search of employment, but the change is more pronounced in conflict. In other cases, women engage in new activities and assume new responsibilities. In Maoist-controlled areas of Nepal, for example, Maoists reported that they provide labor support to farming households headed by widows, especially for those whose male members were killed in the conflict. Women's household and farm-related work burden increased dramatically because male members had left the villages. Traditionally forbidden to plough fields or repair the roofs of houses, women are now taking on these tasks, both out of necessity and because of the more egalitarian value system that the Maoists introduced (CPR 2004). To undertake these new activities, women usually require access to land and other productive resources. Whereas under most customary law systems they are excluded from owning, renting, or inheriting land, during conflict they are regularly allowed access to land to ensure their and their family's survival. However, once the men return, they are often inclined to restore the earlier division of tasks and roles, again taking over activities and responsibilities outside the home, and relegating women to the domestic sphere.

In displacement and often during military service, women and men usually lose access to land and other assets. Displacement exposes them to greater risks as their knowledge base and coping mechanisms may not apply in host areas. They often have to take up alternative livelihood activities for which they are underequipped and untrained. When returning home, women and men must often compete with those who occupied their land and property. When access to land is arranged through the family, and the returnee does not return to the place of origin, the problem becomes even more acute and rural reintegration more complex.[46]

On a more positive note, displacement often forces men, and to a certain degree women, to develop new skills and engage in new income-generating activities, but it has a different impact on men and women. While men have lost their employment opportunities, in certain circumstances, displacement can be empowering for women even when they must continue with their reproductive and parenting tasks. Attempts by males to restrict women's mobility are difficult to enforce in displacement camps, which allows women to gain a wider circle of experiences and establish links with other women's groups. Women may find it easier to engage in petty trade, work that some men may find beneath them. In Georgia, some groups of women were able to conduct trade in citrus fruits and other goods between Abkhazia and Georgia in a manner that men could not, as they were sometimes perceived by Abkhaz authorities as potential guerrillas (Holtzman and Nezam 2004). Women heads represent more than one-third of displaced households in Colombia, many of them widows fleeing with their children after their husband's murder. They appear better able than men to develop support and survival networks after displacement and can often rely on domestic skills to find work as maids or small traders. In contrast, rural men often face higher unemployment rates after displacement because their agricultural skills are of little use in urban environments (Correia 2003; CPR 2004a). In addition, many agencies actively promote women's participation, and donor-supported micro-credit programs often target displaced women and women's associations (e.g., in Eastern and Central Europe). In combination with their loss of any significant role in the public domain, men find it more difficult to adjust to their new positions and the host environment, whereas women appear to be more resilient in camp and host environments (Frerks 2000, quoting Jiggins 1986; Meertens 2001). Interestingly, Turner (1999) finds that a significant number of young men also occupy prominent positions, taking advantage of opportunities offered by humanitarian agencies, NGOs, and politics, as well as a weakening of generational control structures.

The informal urban sector tends to expand in conflict because formal markets and services break down, pushing men and women toward informal income sources. They enter the informal sector more easily and rapidly than the formal sector because it requires less education, training, and capital (ILO 1997, 1998, 2001, 2001a). In many cases, the conflict leads to the closure of large-scale enterprises, and jobs in the public sector may disappear as government services no longer function or, in more extreme cases, the government collapses. War-related employment and "war economies," however, may (partially) offset the decline in formal sector jobs.

Gender-Specific Roles in Urban and Agricultural Work

The major difference between women and men regarding agricultural work is in their access to land, property, housing, credit, labor, and information. Without access to resources, women are economically dependent on their spouses or male relatives and thus vulnerable, especially in the case of divorce, desertion, separation, or widowhood (UNCHS 1999). In theory—i.e., under statutory land tenure systems—women can

---

Box 7.1 Women Faced Discrimination in Land
          Transfer Program

An estimated one-third of the beneficiaries in El Salvador's land transfer program were women. Nevertheless, they experienced widespread discrimination in the program's initial stages. Women FMLN leaders protested on women's behalf, and their presence at the decisionmaking level in the peace negotiations ensured that some problems were subsequently corrected. Ultimately, women did receive land proportional to their FMLN participation. Even so, many women across social classes in both rural and urban areas insist that they were marginalized and faced significant discrimination when reintegration programs were implemented. For example, some local leaders assigned land under the husband's name, and additional criteria that discriminated primarily against women were added for land entitlement, such as literacy and specific documentation (Conaway and Martínez 2004).

---

often own land and property in their own right, but, in practice, customary and traditional practices prevent it. For example, land registration systems may require proof of the husband's authorization for a woman to independently acquire title (UNIFEM 2001). Women may also face additional constraints in accessing land in reconstruction programs, as was the case in El Salvador (see box 7.1). Restrictions in access to credit and lack of farm labor may further limit women's ability to earn agricultural incomes (Bop 2001; Nyirankundabera 2002). In addition, there may be a lack of gender sensitivity in agricultural support services, such as research and extension, or in the promotion of specific crops.

While relatively many women compared to men resort to work in the informal sector (UNDP 2003), their access to formal employment is usually more limited. Women generally seem more willing than men to accept informal sector jobs. Men who previously had a formal sector job may regard informal work as a step back, whereas for women it is often the first and perhaps only option to generate income outside the home. For instance, while it was equally hard for women and men to find formal employment in Georgia, most men remained jobless, whereas women became increasingly active in small-scale trading in markets and bazaars (Morton et al. 2001). Working in the informal sector often reduced women's invisibility and brought them a measure of respect for being able to support the family.

The relatively small number of women who work in the formal sector often lack the same promotion opportunities, remuneration, and rights that men have. In Lebanon, the conflict forced an increasing number of women to work in the formal sector for longer hours and lower wages than their male counterparts (Nauphal 1997). In Bosnia and Herzegovina, where women traditionally worked outside the home, they still suffered employment discrimination through labor laws that did not protect their equal access to employment, and wages that were sometimes only half those of their male counterparts. Women also face problems regarding childcare, maternity leave, and forced early retirement in most parts of Bosnia and Herzegovina (Kumar 2000). Even if countries have legal protections on the books, they are often not enforced.

Dynamics: Changing Labor Market Prospects

Although unequal access to land, property, and other productive resources is not limited to conflict situations, accessing them becomes more complicated or impossible during conflict. Essential infrastructure may have been destroyed or affected by landmines, and women and men may lack access to wage labor (Kumar 2000) or to reciprocal support groups when these are undermined by displacement, divorce or death. The breakdown of markets and services may reduce access to credit and agricultural inputs, which usually remains a problem after conflict. First, access to land becomes a problem in the post-conflict phase when displaced people return and claim land and property, while those who took over their resources do not have alternatives. Second, conflict causes an increase in widows and female-headed households. Widows and children orphaned by conflict represent important vulnerable groups. In Angola, Bosnia and Herzegovina, Kosovo, Mozambique, and Somalia, due to the great number of men who were killed, widows now make up more than half of the population of all adult women. In several war-torn countries in the post-conflict years, more than 70 percent of children depend on widowed mothers as their sole support [UN Department of Economic and Social Affairs (UNDESA) 2001]. In Cambodia and Sudan, there was a 30 percent increase in female-headed households during conflict (El-Bushra et al. 2002; Kumar 2001). Women who are widowed or missing spouses are often not able to inherit or claim their deceased husband's properties (UNIFEM 2001). In some cases (see box 7.2), male relatives rely on custom or power to deny and usurp women's claims to their spouse's rights (UNCHS 1999; Nyirankundabera 2002). In Bosnia and Herzegovina, for example, women returnees and widows faced gender-biased laws and property rights, which considered men

---

Box 7.2 Women's Access to Land Remains an Issue
in Rwanda

The government of Rwanda needed to deal with the staggering number
of landless female household heads after the genocide. A gender desk
was established in parliament, which successfully argued that women
should be given the right to inherit property from their parents or husbands and that widows should be able to reclaim property from their
deceased husband's male relatives. While the process was successful in
institutionalizing support for women's rights, the new law has been difficult to implement at the local level. Traditionalists are loathe to alter
centuries-old customs, and Rwandan women's rights activists warn that
the law will not be effective without a nationwide education campaign
to sensitize women and men (UNIFEM 2001; Rehn and Sirleaf 2002).

---

as the primary landowners (Kvinna till Kvinna 2000). Many women
are rendered homeless and landless after conflict, as previous rental,
ownership, and inheritance systems are reestablished. Ensuring gender
balance in access to land and property often requires fundamental
legal changes.

Gender dynamics in informal employment do not differ much from
those in agriculture. Whereas before conflict many more men than
women work outside the home, conflict forces women and men to find
a job. A kind of "feminization" of the informal employment sector
takes place (Kumar 2001). In the former Yugoslavia, women became
itinerant traders, creating women's networks to transfer money and
goods, exchange homes, and provide jobs and medicines (Slapsak
2001). During the conflict in Somalia, there was a burgeoning of
women petty traders, which led to cooperation among women from
different clans, pooling their resources and strengths, and improving
their coping ability. The number of female petty traders gradually increased because they started educating other women in this form of
business (Byrne 1996, quoting Bennett et al. 1995). After conflict,
many women will continue with their informal activities, often
because they have no other options.

There is little information on whether net formal employment increases or decreases during conflict. On the one hand, state collapse,
closure of enterprises, and interruption of education, health, and other
services lead to a loss of formal employment. On the other hand, the
expansion of security bodies, such as the army and police, and the increase in war-related activities, such as arms manufacturing and trade,

may increase formal employment opportunities. Economic activity may also grow as a consequence of a "war economy" or because the economy operates on a war footing, as was the case in Sri Lanka. And employment opportunities may increase because of economic activities related to the financing of the conflict as in the case of oil, diamonds, and other precious metals (e.g., Angola, Congo-Brazzaville, the DRC, Liberia, Sierra Leone, and Sudan), but the extent to which women and men both benefit from these activities is not clear.

Women's participation in formal employment generally appears to increase during conflict, probably due to war-related activities or the need to replace men engaged in conflict. Women in European countries replaced men in factories and farms during World War II (Bop 2001). In Cambodia, many women started working in factories, and in El Salvador and Guatemala, most employees working in export processing plants were women (Kumar 2001). A USAID study found that female labor force participation rates increased in all the six post-conflict countries studied. Desperate economic conditions and the increase in women-headed households forced greater numbers of women to enter labor markets. Women's participation in agriculture increased in the six countries, except Bosnia (USAID 2001). In Eritrea, as tension along the border with Ethiopia resurfaced in the late 1990s, a Bank report found that the share of women in permanent employment in manufacturing was 56 percent in 1999–01, compared to an average of less than 39 percent for Sub-Saharan Africa. Mobilization into the Eritrean armed forces caused severe labor shortages, which largely explains women's high participation levels in the labor force. Labor shortages were also driving up wages, which had increased by an average of 17 percent, but women suffered from labor market discrimination—male workers earned about 67 percent more than female employees (CPR 2002).

There is little information on women's participation in natural resource sectors that finance conflict, but their benefits likely remain far below those of men; it is unlikely that women play major roles in the production or marketing of minerals (Bop 2001). In one case, however, a woman in Congo-Brazzaville was able to build a successful business when she started to provision the militia in power with fresh food (Bop 2001, quoting Galloy 2000). In Sierra Leone, women in the Lower Bambara Chiefdom, which includes the diamond mining area known as Tongo Field, formed an organization for activities such as vegetable cultivation, for which there was a ready market among alluvial miners (Richards et al. 2004).

The formal employment sector usually expands after conflict as a result of reconstruction activities, the emergence of new sectors such

as tourism, and the presence of a large international community that
at least temporarily needs local staff. While women often lose their
jobs to returning males, particularly ex-soldiers, in other cases they
have succeeded in finding or retaining formal employment after
conflict (see box 7.3).

Box 7.3 Women's Post-Conflict Participation in Formal
Employment Varies

In a number of post-conflict situations such as Angola, Mozambique,
the former Yugoslavia, and Zimbabwe, women faced far more difficulties in entering or staying in formal employment than men,[47] among
other reasons because of the men returning after conflict and the reintroduction of pre-conflict gender relations and labor divisions. The influx of male returnees, including numerous ex-soldiers, meant that
women were generally the first to lose their formal sector jobs, regardless of their position, and that less attention was given to their return to
work. Female ex-soldiers also lost their jobs. According to Bop (2001),
the needs of female soldiers in Sierra Leone and Eritrea were largely
overlooked during reintegration. They remained without a job and lived
in situations of extreme poverty after conflict. In Eritrea, the formal employment sector did not recognize the experiences and skills that women
had gained during conflict and disapproved of the new self-awareness
acquired during conflict. Consequently, women who had had a range of
occupations (barefoot doctors, dentists, administrators, mechanics, and
teachers) during the combat years could not continue their jobs after
conflict (Sörensen 1998).

In other cases, women were encouraged to take up formal employment. In Cambodia, women started working in textile factories, construction, and salt and rubber production during the conflict and have
been working in them ever since. Female workers in textile factories
gained experience as well as a good reputation, which facilitated their
post-conflict employment in the garment industry, where women currently make up more than 80 percent of the work force (Kumar 2001).
In Guatemala, the recovery of tourism provided many women with incomes from the production and sale of crafts (Sörensen 1998). In many
post-conflict situations the presence of a large international community
offered women formal employment opportunities, at least temporarily.
In Bosnia and Herzegovina, many women gained well-paid employment
as interpreters, secretaries, and program assistants, while men worked
as drivers or in lower-pay positions in these organizations because
women were more likely than men to have studied social sciences and
foreign languages (Walsh 1997).

Development Challenges: Capitalizing on Changing Labor Divisions and New Skills

The major challenge is to build on and sustain changes in gender roles that result from conflict (OSCE 2001; Kumar 2001; ILO 2001). Economic assistance programs need to build on women's and men's newly acquired skills, encourage women and men to continue to participate in new economic tasks and activities, and try to ensure more gender balance in accessing productive resources and labor markets.

General Policy Options

Ease Household Burdens that May Limit Participation Outside the Home

Particularly during conflict or shortly thereafter, domestic burdens constrain women's participation in programs that enhance their economic potential. Even if they work outside the home, it often leads to additional burdens because their domestic tasks are not alleviated (e.g., Nauphal 1997). In Guatemala, for instance, the numerous household tasks of returnee women not only hampered their participation in and organization of community activities in the political domain, but also their economic involvement outside the home (Weiss et al. 2001). Agencies can combine the creation of economic opportunities outside the home with efforts to reduce women's daily burden within the household; these can range from laborsaving devices and childcare services to the reconstruction of education, transport, and health facilities (e.g., Royal Tropical Institute 1995). In particular, improving access to fuel and water can have a major impact in freeing up women's time, since these are women's responsibilities in most developing countries. Moreover, when women participate in the selection of community development projects, the demand for water projects often rises—in the Timor-Leste Community Empowerment Project, for example, 29 to 34 percent of funds were used to improve access to clean water (Ostergaard 2003). To assist Chadian women gain incomes outside the home, UNDP, UNIFEM, and local counterparts distributed laborsaving devices such as grinding mills and trained women to manufacture and repair them (Sörensen 1998, quoting Watson 1996).

Anticipate Reproductive and Parenting Tasks

Because of prevailing role divisions, reproductive tasks are an added burden for women who wish to earn a living. In post-conflict El

Salvador, when women were asked about their perceived economic marginalization, they answered that it was because of their many children. With little support from family and social services, women assumed full responsibility for parenting and thus could not take jobs outside the home (Sörensen 1998, quoting Julia 1995). Agencies and local economic actors could minimize this burden by supporting provisions such as childcare and enabling staff to work from the home. In some cases, depending on prevailing social norms and customs, men might be encouraged to share some of the parenting tasks.

Target Women and Men in Economic Assistance without Reinforcing Gender-Stereotyped Labor Divisions

Many agencies realize that women and men often have to be targeted separately in economic assistance programs, such as microcredit and vocational training, to ensure that they benefit equally (Byrne 1996; Sörensen 1998; ICRC 2001). One reason is that women and men undertake different economic activities, and in some cultures women and men do not form one economic unit. For instance, credit, food, and other resources provided to men as household heads may not be shared with their wives and the household, and the income that men generate is not necessarily used to meet basic household needs. To assist women and other household members, they may have to be approached separately from men. However, separate targeting may also reinforce, instead of weaken, gender-stereotypical labor divisions, especially by linking women to informal and men to formal employment. The delicate challenge is not to overlook women or men in economic assistance programs, nor to decrease their chances of equal participation in all employment sectors.

Develop a Long-Term, Integrated Approach toward Gender and Employment

More gender-balanced economic participation will only be achieved if economic changes are complemented with changes in the legal framework, customary law, family institutions, and traditions. Besides creating new employment opportunities, providing microcredit or improving access to land, there is a need to educate and sensitize key actors such as legislators, judges, employers, communities, and traditional leaders about gender issues regarding work (OSCE 2001). While in theory women and men may have equal labor rights, in practice prevailing social norms often prevent them from being realized (Kumar 2001).

Rural Policy Options

Provide Women and Men with the Means to Survive

The short-term objective of most economic assistance programs is to restore livelihoods and, where possible, to help women and men regain economic self-sufficiency. They generally involve: (i) distribution of agricultural inputs and tools, small livestock, and other materials; (ii) technical advice and skills training; (iii) microcredit programs, often targeted to rural areas or disadvantaged groups; and (iv) restoration of communal assets through mine-clearing or repairing roads, houses, and bridges (Bouta and Frerks 2002, quoting ILO 1998). Implementation modalities depend on the nature of the task (quick-impact, short-term, rehabilitation, or longer-term development) and the agency's characteristics and mandate.

The key challenge is to target and involve women and men equally. A basic lesson is that, without making additional efforts to reach women, they will be overlooked. A prior step should be a context-specific gender analysis, which can examine whether women require different assistance and how to reach them. Other options include involving women's organizations in distributing assistance to women and other vulnerable groups, including men, and focusing on the assistance channels, for instance, involving women in mine-awareness activities by distributing material through food distribution points where women are generally in the majority (ICRC 2001), or other channels such as community centers, hospitals, schools, and childcare facilities.

Ensure Equal Access to Land and Other Productive Assets[48]

Agencies can consider helping women and men to inherit and own productive assets, especially land. They can encourage enshrinement of property rights, ownership, and entitlements in legislation, including statutory and nonstatutory laws. Once these are enshrined, they can help to enforce legislation, for instance, by establishing and supporting legal aid services that make women and men aware of their rights (see box 7.4).

In addition to more equal access to land, women and men need access to other resources, including transportation, extension services, credit, and markets [OSCE 2001; Food and Agriculture Organization (FAO) 2002; Farr 2002]. Anecdotal evidence from Rwanda suggests that where women had access to land, it often did not improve their economic empowerment because they lacked

---

Box 7.4 Women Face a Post-Conflict Struggle for Land Access and Ownership

Upon their return to Guatemala, refugee women who were officially granted co-ownership of land were prevented by (their) men from using and owning the land because of the reintroduction of patriarchal relationships (Weiss Fagen and Yudelman 2001; Worby 2001). Women in Bosnia and Herzegovina faced gender-biased laws on property rights and required legal assistance by a local NGO to improve access to and ownership of land and property upon their return (Kvinna till Kvinna 2000). Rwandan women were prevented from owning and inheriting property, but this changed with the 1999 Rwanda Inheritance Law, which granted equal inheritance rights to male and female children and established a choice of property regimes upon marriage, allowing a wife to inherit her deceased husband's property. Despite this substantial improvement, women, particularly in the Rwandan countryside, cannot yet access land because of the prevailing customary system in which male household heads control access to land.

---

access to credit and manpower (Nyirankundabera 2002). Since equal land rights will probably not be enshrined quickly, access to resources will be women's first need, especially for female-headed households.

Gender-Sensitize Agricultural Support Services

The way in which support services are designed and channeled can have important gender implications. In Sierra Leone, access to agricultural technology remains more limited for women. A World Bank Gender Assessment for Sierra Leone found that of the 1,500 extension workers, only 30 were women, making it difficult for women farmers to have direct access to information—direct contact with male extension workers is not welcomed. The assessment also found that post-conflict efforts to rehabilitate the agricultural sector, which include distributing tools and seeds using a household approach, militate against married women. Women and men often farm different fields (and different crops), but since the husband as head of the household receives the tools and seeds, he often diverts them to his own field. Catholic Relief Services attempted to get around this problem by offering male and female farmers vouchers through which they could access tools and seeds, though no impact evaluation was available (World Bank 2003). Richards et al. (2004) relate that when

---

Box 7.5 Women's Organizations Are Revived in Rwanda

There was a substantial reemergence of women's organizations in Rwanda after 1994. The urgency of women's needs, the tradition of community organization, and government and donor support were important in reviving these organizations. Groups of rural women, for example, built on previous rural organizations that had provided economic and social support to their members. After the conflict, they helped to address the needs of women and other vulnerable groups and were involved in rehabilitation, including house construction, distribution of small livestock and agricultural tools, as well as providing microcredit to encourage income-generating activities (Newbury and Baldwin 2001; Sörensen 1998).

CARE in Sierra Leone decided to offer seeds to all adults, and not via household heads (as it had done previously), it was surprised to discover the extent to which seed requirements changed. Offered an independent choice, the women's (and young men's) requests for groundnut seeds rose compared to rice. Groundnuts in Sierra Leone are recognized as a woman's crop, which also has important empowering potential since it offers women the possibility of engaging in petty trading.

Revive Self-Help Groups

Women and men can gain better access to income opportunities and re-sources through self-help groups, which largely consist of women in many conflict-affected situations. Especially in agriculture, women's and some men's self-help groups have played important post-conflict roles in guaranteeing land and property rights, mobilizing resources, re-creating a sense of community, and helping one another with agricultural tasks. This has been noted in Angola, Chad, Eritrea, Liberia, Rwanda, and Sierra Leone (Sörensen 1998). The groups often exist before conflict, but stop functioning during conflict and need to be revived (see box 7.5).

Informal Sector Policy Options

Working in the informal sector is not always a matter of choice. Conflict forces many men and women to accept low-paying work in the informal sector simply to survive, as other alternatives may have disappeared. Besides capitalizing on women's and men's newly gained experiences, skills, and networks, agencies can help to avoid negative aspects often associated with informal sector work, such as low pay, long working hours, lack of labor rights, and other legal protections. The following policy options should be considered:

Deal Critically with Microcredit Programs

Often targeted to women, quick-impact microcredit programs have brought much-needed relief after conflict. Although these programs clearly benefit women, some have questioned whether their participation in microcredit programs may be at the expense of greater efforts to involve them in larger economic assistance programs, such as a revival of manufacturing or large infrastructure works (Rehn and Sirleaf 2002). Although there is no evidence to support this concern, it does reinforce the need to ensure that women and men have equal opportunities to participate in and benefit from larger economic assistance programs.

Also, the economic sustainability and empowerment potential of microcredit programs are often limited (ILO 1998; ICRC 2001; Kumar 2001). They may kick-start income-generating activities, but they usually need to be complemented by other forms of support, especially training in business practices and market skills (Sörensen 1998). Low repayment rates also frequently constrain the financial sustainability of such programs, although it should be noted that women generally have much higher repayment rates than men and manage to repay credit on time (SIDA 2000). Another lesson is that providing credit to solidarity groups rather than to individuals may also increase the chances of repayment and may contribute to revitalizing social relations and building social capital (Baden 1997; ILO 1998, 2001; Oklahoma 1999). Some of these experiences are noted below (see box 7.6).

The Pros and Cons of Vocational Training Programs

Most vocational training programs include training in skills, businesses, management, and marketing. Because of high competition in the informal labor market, vocational training programs have often contributed to market saturation and thus limited income-generation potential. Therefore each program should be based on an analysis of employment opportunities and existing skills, taking into account newly acquired gender roles. Women's training programs should be as market-oriented and business-minded as those for men and not only focus on low-paid, gender-stereotyped occupations (see box 7.7), as is

Box 7.6 Women Can Benefit from Microcredit Programs

In post-conflict Cambodia, microcredit lending has been one of the most important activities of women's organizations. Loans are usually provided to a group of three to seven members who are collectively responsible for ensuring repayment. In the absence of formal lending and banking institutions, such programs have been popular with women—women are almost 95 percent of the participants in group lending programs. These programs have helped many women to initiate small income-generating projects such as farming, poultry raising, and petty trade (Kumar and Baldwin 2001).

Donors and women's organizations in Georgia have cooperated on microcredit lending for female traders. The Norwegian Refugee Council supported a women's organization, Women in Business, to create a small-business revolving fund for up to 1,000 clients, with the ultimate goal of transforming it into a self-sustaining credit union. Beginning with 100 lari ($50) loans at 3 percent interest with six-month terms, the loans increase in number and volume as they are repaid. Although still in its early stages, the scheme has had close to a 100 percent repayment rate. Save the Children worked with the women's organization Constanta, which provides low-interest loans to groups of internally displaced female traders. By spring 1999, Constanta had a loan portfolio of nearly 220,000 lari, 2,480 clients, and a loan default rate below 2 percent (Morton et al. 2001).

In Eritrea, the major problem faced by women participating in ACORD's savings and credit scheme was a lack of ideas on how to invest funds. ACORD's response was to include training in business skills and to involve barefoot bankers to counsel and encourage women to participate, especially female ex-combatants (Sörensen 1998; de Watteville 2002). The barefoot bankers, half of them female ex-fighters, also helped to assess the viability of proposed projects and provided advice during implementation (Bruchhaus and Mehreteab 2000).

Women's communal funds were established in Rwanda in 1997. Women had to contribute a nominal amount to demonstrate will and commitment; once a certain amount was collected, local women's committees could request funds from the Ministry of Gender and Women in Development. The funds were channeled to the local level for housing, clothing, livestock, and agricultural inputs. However, women complained that the loan size was insufficient to maintain a store or to expand into more profitable activities, which suggests that the longer-term economic empowering effects may be somewhat limited (WCRWC 2001; UNDP/UNIFEM 2002).

Box 7.7 Vocational Training Programs for Women Are
          Found Lacking

A number of post-conflict skills training and employment promotion
programs in Mozambique set up sewing classes for women, despite the
obvious limitations as a source of livelihood. Only a few instances of
nontraditional training for women were identified, such as in the Active
Employment Center in Inhambane, where women were trained in panel
beating, plumbing, and other nontraditional skills.[49] Other training such
as food processing, administrative and managerial skills, tourism, and
commerce would also assist women's participation in Mozambique's
labor market (Baden 1997).

In Guatemala, UNICEF sponsored courses on dressmaking, textiles,
crafts, embroidery, hairdressing, and cake decoration, leading to work
in the informal sector. The range of projects, however, was too narrow,
which resulted in crowding, duplication of products, and uncompetitive
businesses. Micro-businesses were also failing because women lacked
training in business skills, including accounts, pricing, marketing strategies, and production techniques and standards (Date-Bah and Walsh
2001).

The U.S. government–funded Bosnian Women's Initiative, that
UNHCR administered, included a variety of vocational projects for
women; these largely focused on gender-stereotyped trades such as
sewing, knitting, typing, and hairdressing. Market saturation in these
fields made them less competitive and less profitable.[50]

An independent evaluation of the U.S. government–funded Kosovo
Women's Initiative (KWI) that UNHCR and IRC administered suggests
that these lessons were not internalized. A widely heard criticism of the
KWI vocational projects referred to the multitude of sewing, hairdressing, and English-language courses. The prevailing view was that, while
many of these projects were beneficial in group formation and trauma relief during the emergency phase, there was little sustainability planning.
Although there were some successful attempts to diversify into nontraditional activities, success required careful preparation, including
market research and a gender equity analysis (Baker and Haug 2002).

---

often the case (Royal Tropical Institute 1995; ILO 1998). In addition,
agencies must assess how much skills and business training women
and men need before they can apply them in practice. While some programs helped develop some competencies, they were often too short,
too small-scale, and too little profit-oriented.

To ensure more gender-balanced participation, it is also important
to involve women and men in decisions regarding location, facilities

(e.g., childcare), and program schedules (ILO 1997, 1998, 2001). In particular, providing childcare improves women's ability to participate in vocational programs and other activities outside the home. Governments would usually be responsible for establishing childcare services, but this is not realistic in countries with limited resources and inadequate public and social services. In Rwanda, for example, ICRC encouraged women in the community to cope with childcare themselves (ICRC 2001). The ILO experience suggests that community-based training programs, which enable on-site childcare facilities, have been successful (ILO 1998). In Eritrea, ACORD and women from the agency responsible for demobilization and reintegration, Mitias, built a childcare center in the town of Keren, which not only increased women's mobility in searching for a job, but also created temporary employment for a large number of women. It allowed women to acquire skills that enabled them to enter the male-dominated construction sector and demonstrated that women are able to build houses on their own (BICC 2002).

Focus on Improving Labor Conditions

Given men's and especially women's limited scope for employment outside the informal sector, it is important to try to improve the conditions under which they work. Although this is already a huge challenge in the formal sector, it is even more difficult in the informal sector. The literature reviewed did not touch upon this topic, but agencies could explore the extent to which labor rights and social protection systems could be extended to the informal sector (adapted from OSCE 2001).

Formal Sector Policy Options

An option to improve women's access to formal employment is to carefully consider some form of affirmative action. While this may be a starting point to compensate for low female participation in the formal sector, there is a risk that men will feel disadvantaged and women become stigmatized in the long run as being unable to enter the formal sector without external assistance. Another risk is that it will contribute to gender-stereotyped labor relations.

Encourage Employment in Traditional Women's Sectors

Various sectors have traditionally employed relatively large numbers of women, such as education, health, and the civil service. Sensitization campaigns and incentives directed at employers to hire women (de Watteville 2002) could increase the acceptance of women working in these sectors (ILO 2001), although the authors did not come across practical evidence regarding this option in post-conflict settings. In the Netherlands, for instance, there is some evidence that such incentives have worked to stimulate women's reentry into the labor force and employment of the partially disabled. Whether this is applicable to conflict and post-conflict situations needs to be further explored. A possible example may be Eritrea, where the government practiced positive discrimination toward ex-fighters, substantially benefiting female ex-combatants. It provided 310 ex-fighters (three-quarters of them women) with a license to distribute beer and liquor and sold 49 minibuses on credit to a company of 208 shareholders composed mainly of women and war-disabled fighters. The company created jobs for 250 people, mainly ex-fighters (Bruchhaus and Mehreteab 2000). In addition, refresher courses for women and men who had to give up their jobs can help to update their skills and regain their jobs.

Certify Existing Skills and Experiences

Many women develop new skills and gain new working experiences during conflict, which makes them more competitive in post-conflict labor markets. The main obstacle, however, is that women, but also many men, usually do not have the diplomas and certificates to show their qualifications. The Ethiopian Commission for the Rehabilitation of Members of the Former Army and Disabled War Veterans issued certificates to 7,908 ex-soldiers—out of 158,710 ex-soldiers in the urban target group—to facilitate the employment of soldiers who acquired marketable skills in the military. Among other things, certificates were issued for technical, electrical, driving, and construction occupations (Colletta et al. 1996). The need for certification was also raised in the reintegration of female ex-combatants in Eritrea (Barth 2002). Agencies can support local institutions to conduct such certification programs (OSCE 2001; de Watteville 2002; Barth 2002).

Undertake Positive Actions to Involve Women in Rehabilitation and Development Activities

As suggested previously, agencies may consider actively involving women and women's organizations in post-conflict rehabilitation and development programs. Women's participation could be encouraged in those activities that have greater impact on their lives. For instance, the rehabilitation of schools, hospitals, pit latrines, wells, and other community services may impact women more than men because they reduce women's domestic burden. In addition, skills they acquire and

---

Box 7.8 Gender Analysis Identifies Measures to Increase
Female Participation

Gender analysis of the Feeder Roads Program (FRP), a labor-intensive
public works program in Mozambique, was useful in identifying constraints on female participation and proposing measures to address
them. The FRP, which had as its main objective the rehabilitation and
maintenance of tertiary roads, also aimed to generate temporary employment during rehabilitation and, to a lesser extent, to create a number of permanent road maintenance jobs. It aimed to employ 25 percent
women, but when women still made up only 14 percent of employees, a
midterm evaluation called for additional measures, such as gender sensitization and staff training, targeted strategies, coordination with existing women's organizations, clear recruitment guidelines, provision of
health care, and access to food and childcare facilities (Baden 1997; ILO
1998). Actions were taken to implement the findings, but no evaluation
was available to assess impact.

---

use in rehabilitation programs can be more diverse and usually have
greater market value than "traditional female skills" (see box 7.8).

Improve Basic Employment Conditions for Women and Men

Support can include: gender-sensitizing labor and other relevant laws,
raising awareness among employers and state officials to improve
women's access to employment, addressing gender-stereotypical labor
roles, and reducing discrimination and sexual harassment on the work
floor. It could also relate to the length of workdays, part-time labor opportunities, equal salaries for women and men, women's rights and employment protection, childcare facilities, and maternal or parental leave
(Loufti 2001). Local organizations such as labor ministries and trade
unions should be involved in these efforts (ILO 1998; SIDA 2000).

CHAPTER 8

Gender and Rehabilitating Social Services: A Focus on Education

IN ALL SITUATIONS, WOMEN AND MEN need adequate nutrition, safe drinking water, protection from violence, and access to health care and education, but these needs are greater in conflict settings. Conflict has direct effects on health, causing disease, disabilities, injuries, psychological stress, trauma, and death, but also indirect effects. Water and food may become scarce, leading to malnutrition, famine, and the spread of diseases. Health facilities may be destroyed, health workers killed or displaced, administrative capacities and systems eroded, and investments and programs in the health sector (e.g., immunization campaigns) halted (Rehn and Sirleaf 2002). For the same reasons, education and training facilities often stop functioning during conflict (ILO 1998). This chapter analyzes gender aspects in the rehabilitation of social services, with a particular focus on education. It touches only lightly on the health sector—primary health care, basic reproductive health, and psychological support—as chapter 3 addresses the gender dimensions of health sector rehabilitation that emerge due to GBV, psychosocial needs, and HIV/AIDS. Moreover, although the health sector's post-conflict rehabilitation is clearly a priority and a complex undertaking, the authors did not find many references in the literature to additional gender dimensions in this area. Gender dynamics, on the other hand, are a critical dimension in the complex interaction between education and conflict.

Overview

In most conflict situations, *gender-specific roles* dictate that women become the primary home providers of health care and education. While women's regular household tasks become more complex during conflict, they often also become responsible for providing health care to ill, old, and injured family and community members. In addition, some women also provide childcare and home schooling for their children during conflict. On the one hand, this key *gender role change* considerably increases women's burden of dependency, but it may also strengthen women's skills and organizational capabilities, inducing them to take on more public roles during or after conflict.

From a development perspective, the first *key challenge* is to try to keep health and education facilities functioning during conflict; the post-conflict challenge is to restore and reshift these services from the private to the public domain as soon as possible. Another challenge is to further gender-sensitize post-conflict education and health services. Agencies need to try to ensure that services become more equally accessible for women and men and that they take both their educational and physical needs into account better.

Although conflict's overall impact on education systems is unambiguously negative, the collapse of centralized and inefficient systems and the attendant shift from the public to the private domain provide scope for major reforms in the post-conflict period; it presents a good opportunity to gender-sensitize the education system. This window of opportunity, however, tends to be brief as education systems can recover very quickly, and vested interests and pre-conflict social norms are also quickly reestablished.

Reshifting education and health care services in a post-conflict society may take a long time. One policy option for this transformation phase is to start changing the perception that men's and particularly women's health and education work are a natural extension of domestic work and not a professional occupation. Agencies could start challenging this perception, for instance, by contracting women to work in educational and medical rehabilitation projects. Another policy option is to support community- and home-based schooling and health care facilities, where usually many women are involved, as a first step toward reconstructing the formal systems. Options to gender-sensitize health systems may focus on the provision of basic health care, reproductive health care, and psychological assistance to conflict survivors. Additional expertise is normally needed to handle issues such as war-induced handicaps and disabilities, GBV, STD and HIV/AIDS prevention and treatment, abortion, rape, and other post-conflict traumas. To gender-sensitize education, agencies could pay more attention to adult education, particularly for women, and to girls' high dropout rates for school during and after conflict. Finally, they could support the development of nondiscriminatory education and training, for instance, by eliminating gender stereotyping from education materials, incorporating gender issues in teachers' pre- and in-service training, and educating government officials in gender issues.

Gender-Specific Roles and Needs

The lack of health care facilities and of basic services for water, transportation, energy, housing, and sanitation tends to affect women more than men. First, during conflict service provision often shifts from the public to the private domain and becomes the responsibility of women and mothers. After conflict, the resumption of public services reduces women's burdens in the household and enables them to retake their normal daily activities, including income-generating activities where possible (Bouta and Frerks 2002). Second, a number of gender-specific differences in health relate to women's and men's different physiologies. For example, women are more vulnerable to vitamin and iron deficiencies and thus to malnutrition than are men. Coping mechanisms may also play a role, where women reduce their own intake to provide food for their husbands and dependents, worsening the already inequitable food distribution in households and the community (UN 2002). These differences exist in situations of stability, but tend to be exacerbated during conflict. Third, women require additional security and health care services to meet their gynecological and reproductive health needs. They are more vulnerable to diseases and need specific forms of nutrition and support during and after pregnancy. These needs occur in both conflict and nonconflict situations, but during conflict women may have less resistance, while access to services is harder. For example, dangerous birthing practices and the lack of access to midwives resulted in higher death rates for women and adolescent girls during the Sierra Leone conflict (Rehn and Sirleaf 2002). More women than men are affected by GBV and this increases during conflict; many women also suffer from injuries, infections, unwanted pregnancies, sexual dysfunction, and HIV/AIDS and from mental problems such as anxiety, post-traumatic stress disorders, and depression, which sometimes leads to suicide (adapted from Rehn and Sirleaf 2002).

While the manifestation of gender aspects varies considerably from context to context, it plays a critical role in the link between education and conflict. There is evidence that—even if schools remain open—the drop in female enrollment is higher in times of war (UN 2002). During conflicts, girls frequently have to take on unconventional roles in the family and help female household heads cope with their family's survival needs. Getting to and from school becomes even more challenging during conflict in terms of security (Education Team 2003). As Sommers (2002) points out, an irony surrounding education in war-affected areas is that, although conflicts may force boys to be mobile and girls to settle and reduce their mobility, it is girls who are usually much less likely to attend school. This is the case even in refugee camp settings where agencies set up education programs targeted to girls. In some situations, girls are kept out of school less because of their responsibilities elsewhere or the low social value placed on their education than because avoiding school is seen as a protection measure against sexual abuse and early pregnancy. What is clear from the literature and available data is that in most cases, girls are at a significant disadvantage in conflict-affected countries in terms of access to primary education, and this disadvantage is usually much higher at the secondary and higher levels (Education Team 2003).

Education is also a primary channel through which a particular identity, set of values, and world view are transmitted. As such, the formal education system is a powerful avenue for promoting respect for human rights and building social cohesion—it can also undermine social cohesion and create or reinforce social divisions and patterns of exclusion. High poverty levels among female-headed families are a factor in girls' low enrollment, but so is their social marginalization. Although there is no lack of evidence on conflict's damaging impact on education systems, less well understood is the role that education systems and schooling frequently play in reproducing the attitudes, values, and social relations (including gender) that underlie civil conflict and violence in the first place. Education systems and schools are widely expected to play a role in mediating the relationship between ethnic and religious groups and in building social capital, but they can also be manipulated to exacerbate these cleavages. Textbooks in particular—the most influential artifact of the curriculum process—can carry implicit messages as well as explicit biases, including tacit acceptance of violence as a way of resolving issues, and promote images of militarized masculinities. Conflict has the effect of eroding society's core values, as children are orphaned, recruited, or separated from their parents, as teachers and children are traumatized by violence, as education systems and curricula become politicized, and as a culture of violence is reflected in school practices and even textbooks (adapted from Education Team 2003).

Dynamics: Complex Interactions but Also Opportunities

In most conflict situations gender-specific roles dictate that women become the primary home health care providers. During conflict women's household tasks become more complex and numerous, but often they also become responsible for providing health care to extended family and community members and face increased risks of communicable diseases and epidemics. Also, women often provide childcare and home schooling to their children during conflict.[51] A more positive effect is that women may strengthen their skills and organizational capabilities, which motivates them to organize and take on more public roles during or after conflict.

In the education sector, gender dynamics are complex. While a significant number of conflict-affected countries report high gender inequities in access to primary and especially higher education levels, these inequities can be found in many countries not affected by conflict. The case of Angola is illustrative (Education Team 2003). Gender inequities during the conflict favored men in both rural and urban areas. In urban areas, the percentage of women who did not complete the fourth grade was four times higher than for men. The gender gap in access to education was consistently in favor of boys throughout the war. Although it narrowed slightly from around 13 percent in 1991 to as low as 7 percent in 1997, it was largely the result of a more rapid decline in boys' enrollment, rather than net gains by girls. In 1998, with a rapid return to school with the hope of peace, the gap opened again as boys flooded back to school at a faster rate than girls, only to revert to the previous pattern when the peace initiative collapsed at the end of 1998. A number of World Bank country studies provide examples where the primary enrollment gender gap actually declines during conflict, usually as more boys are drawn into conflict. For example, despite its long-standing conflict, Colombia has made significant progress in reducing gender inequalities in education (and health), although this is largely influenced by a deterioration in the status of males. Colombian boys have worse completion, educational attainment, dropout, and repetition rates than girls, and these have been exacerbated by the crisis. Males are also more affected by HIV/AIDS, alcohol, and drug-related deaths (Correia 2003). The case of Burundi shows that the closing of the gender gap is a consequence not of increased access by girls but a greater decline in boys' enrollment. It should be noted, however, that as the declining conflict level permits more children to return to school, the gender gap opens again to almost the same level as before the conflict (Education Team 2003).

There is also some limited evidence that conflict may reduce the age when females marry. In a sample of isolated villages in Sierra Leone, Richards et al. (2004) found that the average marriage age was lower for those marrying in the past decade than for those that married two to three decades ago—between 1.6 and 0.9 years lower. They suggest that this likely reflects a lack of education opportunities for girls.

Although conflict's overall impact on education systems is unambiguously negative, the collapse of centralized and often inefficient

Box 8.1 Community Education Fills the Schooling Gap during Conflict

In El Salvador and Guatemala, as the official education system abandoned the most strife-torn rural areas, some local and spontaneous education structures emerged. El Salvador's *Escuelas Populares*, set up in regions where the fighting was fiercest, were run largely by communities and local educators, many of whom had completed only two grades of basic education themselves. The main aim of these schools, often supported by foreign NGOs and churches, was to teach local children to read and write. Nontraditional community schooling also took shape in Guatemala. These included facilities set up in "resistance communities," whose residents had fled or been driven from their homes. In some remote communities, regular teachers or community educators provided instruction as best they could under dangerous circumstances and as hostilities raged on around them (Marques and Bannon 2003). Although these experiences have not been evaluated from a gender perspective, anecdotal evidence especially in El Salvador suggests that community-based education reforms provide an opportunity for women (and men) to gain greater voice and develop organizational capabilities in their communities, often extending beyond educational issues.

systems and the attendant shift from the public to the private domain do provide some scope for major reforms in the post-conflict period. During conflict, previously highly centralized education systems tend to fragment as the capacity of the central authorities is stretched and/or their legitimacy is questioned. As the formal education system weakens or collapses, alternative education structures can emerge as communities mobilize to take on the task of organizing their children's education, sometimes with the support of rebel movements and NGOs (see box 8.1). Parental involvement in running local schools is a potentially important way of building skills in community participation, especially for women. As Richards et al. (2004) point out in the case of Sierra Leone, there are few other occasions for which the rural poor—especially young mothers—will prioritize time to attend meetings concerning school business that directly affects their own children's welfare.

Although conflict severely impacts primary education systems, these systems are surprisingly resilient and can recover rapidly following conflict. The secondary and tertiary systems appear far less resilient. For example, although Sierra Leone was seriously affected by the conflict, it was able to report very substantial primary enrollment growth within two years after the conflict had ended. In Timor-Leste, where primary enrollment rates were restored very rapidly to levels above those prevalent before the conflict, there was far less progress in enrollment rates at the secondary and tertiary levels (Education Team 2003). In Rwanda, World Bank estimates show that only five years after the conflict ended, the number of primary school students had rebounded to its pre-genocide long-term trend line. Rwanda's gross primary enrollment ratio, at 107 percent today, is higher than in other sub-Saharan countries at similar income levels. While there are issues of quality (including high repetition rates), and much of the loss in human capital (due to deaths, injuries, and permanent school dropouts) cannot be recouped, the country may well be on track to meet key Millennium Development Goals (CPR 2004b). In Afghanistan, through extraordinary efforts that the international community supported, more than 3 million children were enrolled in school in 2002 and more than 4 million in 2003, one-third of them girls. Girls' gross primary enrollment rate was an impressive 40 percent in 2003, compared to a prewar (1974) rate of only 9 percent (World Bank 2004).

Development Challenges: Sustained, Gender-Sensitive Services

It is important to try to ensure that health and education services are kept functioning during conflict and restored as soon as possible after conflict. Post-conflict education systems must not only increase human capital, but also have the potential to strengthen social relations, to support peace and reconciliation, and to sensitize policymakers, teachers, and students to gender issues. Health systems need to respond to basic and reproductive health care and provide psychological assistance to conflict survivors. They should broaden their expertise to handle war injuries, handicaps, disabilities, GBV, STD and HIV/AIDS prevention and treatment, abortion, and post-conflict trauma. This requires gender sensitivity because of women and men's different health needs. During conflict, humanitarian agencies provide most of these services. The question is what role developing agencies can play in the social sector's rehabilitation and what medium- and longer-term developments they should support. An immediate challenge is to reactivate public services, which can reduce household pressures on women. The longer-term challenge is to gender-sensitize the education and health services that are being rehabilitated.

The education sector presents particular opportunities and challenges. The opportunities arise because given the devastation wrought by conflict and the priority assigned to it by communities, the advent of peace offers an opportunity for wide-ranging education reforms and to undo the errors of the past. At the same time, this window of opportunity is brief as education systems recover quickly and vested interests and social mores become quickly entrenched (CPR 2004c). Thus, attempts to rebuild more gender-balanced education systems must be undertaken quickly to resist the reversal to social and education gender biases in pre-conflict settings.

Policy Options

Restart Public Education and Health Services

States usually face a major challenge in reestablishing public services during the post-conflict transitional period. The provision of education and health services in the immediate post-conflict phase often relies on unpaid work, taken up by men and especially women as an extension of their household tasks or through community mobilization. Anecdotal evidence suggests that community-based organizations, which include many women, have been instrumental in rehabilitating schools and health clinics. Studies on Eritrea, Ethiopia, and Rwanda, for instance, show that women, particularly because of their extended social networks, played an important role in rehabilitating schools and health clinics (Sörensen 1998). Options for external support in this transitional phase are to:

- *Value professionally women's and men's efforts.* Women's health and education work is often perceived as a natural extension of domestic work and not as a professional occupation. Changing this perception would likely increase women's access to training and remuneration, as well as the status and respect that their work entails (Sörensen 1998). Whereas there is probably a limited role for agencies in changing such perceptions, they could start by challenging these perceptions through information and sensitization campaigns and by contracting women in education and health rehabilitation projects.
- *Take community- or home-based education and health systems as a starting point.* Agencies could assess how to support community- and home-based schooling and health care facilities as a basis on which to rebuild the formal systems (see box 8.2). El Salvador's community-based education model (EDUCO) is a good example.

Box 8.2 Home-Schooling Girls in Afghanistan Addresses
Educational Needs

In Afghanistan there is evidence that clandestine, home-based schooling
initiatives, which flourished during the Taliban regime, were particularly effective in addressing girls' educational needs. It is likely that
educated urban families will want to see their daughters educated in formal girls' schools. However, for more conservative and traditional families, particularly refugees from a rural background who are increasingly
settling in urban centers and who have had no prior exposure to education, the availability of a more "secluded" educational environment
may help to improve the uptake of education by girls (ILO 2001).

- *Employ women and men in the health and education sectors'*
  reconstruction. Many men, and especially women, have gained
  informal experience in teaching and health care. Agencies may
  employ them, for instance, in health care programs, training, and
  discussion groups on health-related issues. This could be a first
  step toward longer-term employment (Sörensen 1998).

Gender-Sensitizing Health and Education Services

Most policy options to gender-sensitize health systems in conflict situations were discussed in chapter 3, above, but they are also helpful to
gender-sensitize health services at large. Moreover, development agencies can derive lessons and best practices from the humanitarian assistance field, for instance, regarding the provision of counseling to GBV
survivors, of reproductive health care services, of specialized facilities
to deal with war injuries, and of preventive health care, particularly
with regard to HIV/AIDS and other STDs.[52] Efforts to gender-sensitize
post-conflict education should include:

- *Broadening the focus beyond primary education* (ICRC 2001).
  Women in particular often sacrifice their own education for that
  of their children, at times having to choose between their own
  education and their family's survival. WFP addressed this issue in
  Eritrea by launching the Food for Training Program. The program provided women and some men who attended a two-hour
  daily literacy course with a food parcel to compensate them for
  the time they would have spent preparing food for their families.
  These types of initiatives can also be applied to vocational programs and other forms of assistance. Agencies should also assess

the scope for providing adult education without negatively influencing primary education; they should consider not only basic literacy and numeracy courses, but also combining these with workshops on entrepreneurship, gender equality, human rights, and peace education. Medica Zenica in Bosnia and Herzegovina established an education center for women and girls whose education was interrupted during the war. It offered individual counseling and the opportunity to complete high school education or vocational training courses (Rehn and Sirleaf 2002).

- *Encouraging more equal participation of women and men, girls and boys.* It is outside the scope of this review to analyze the many initiatives undertaken in nonconflict situations to improve female education and access to education. These initiatives, however, also need to be applied in conflict situations. A particular concern in post-conflict situations is the high dropout rates as a result of lack of money for school books, clothes, or fees, in addition to the need for the labor of adolescents and girls in the household. Ways to prevent and reduce such dropout rates need to be explored, for example, by providing support to families where children work at home or by encouraging dropouts to return to school by visiting them personally (OSCE 2001). In Sierra Leone, women mobilized their own resources to rebuild schools destroyed during the war to help ensure their children's education, particularly for girls (UN 2002). In Rwanda, women's organizations centered their efforts on educating girls, for instance, by organizing workshops and media programs to raise awareness of girls' education. They also launched a research program to determine why girls drop out of school and to develop an action program to sensitize girls and their parents to the importance of girls continuing their studies (Newbury and Baldwin 2001).

- *Prioritizing the education of rural girls.* Expansion of access that prioritizes girls, poor communities, and rural areas can be an effective way of rapidly closing gender gaps. However, education targeting rural girls must be adapted to rural conditions. As Richards et al. (2004) point out in the case of Sierra Leone, even though girls' basic education is a right and is not to be defended solely on utilitarian grounds, parents must still be convinced. A village school offering reasonable quality education—especially where this provides skills that translate into rural life—allows parents more of a sliding scale of response and less often an all-or-nothing choice between education and access to a daughter's labor power through marriage alliances.

- *Developing nondiscriminatory education and training.* Options include eliminating gender stereotypes from education materials, especially the curriculum, to including gender issues in teachers' pre- and in-service training and training government officials in gender issues (OSCE 2001). Curriculum reform is often a key first step in a process that proceeds in stages. During the early stages, curriculum reform is usually limited to sanitizing the curricula and textbooks of biased content or stereotypes. Substantive curriculum reform can usually only get under way in reconstruction's later stages, as well as through training teachers to impart the revised curriculum and teaching approaches (adapted from Education Team 2003). These efforts are important in nonconflict situations, but the post-conflict reconstruction phase offers an opportunity for more comprehensive reforms, which should include engendering the education system. Teaching materials for peace education also need to consider the different war experiences of women and men, as well as the renegotiated gender roles of women and men throughout conflict (UN 2002).

CHAPTER 9

Gender and Community-Driven Development

Overview

THE EROSION OF SOCIAL CAPITAL is one of the legacies of violent and prolonged intrastate conflict. Once the conflict ends, even if other forms of capital (human, financial, or physical) can be replenished, sustainable development will be constrained unless positive social capital can also be rebuilt. Rebuilding social capital and cohesion are deeply *gendered* processes, even though they are still described in a nongendered manner. Post-conflict development efforts increasingly emphasize participatory and CDD processes to strengthen social cohesion and build bridging social capital. A major potential *change* is that the adoption of community-driven approaches to post-conflict reconstruction can encourage more gender-balanced representation in local decisionmaking processes and, if sustained, provide a springboard for greater women's empowerment and involvement in broader political processes.

A *key development challenge* is to address factors that constrain women's participation in local community development efforts and their representation in decisionmaking structures and processes. *Policy options* include adopting community-based approaches in reconstruction, mobilizing the support of men and the community as a whole to support women's participation, investing in training community leaders and gender facilitators, adapting timing and logistics to women's needs, and ensuring strong monitoring and evaluation. In addition, women's participation can be evaluated within broader and more contextualized social processes—moving beyond simple gender rules for attendance and voting—which often mask more complex cleavages based on class, lineages, religion, or ethnicity.

Gender Aspects of Social Capital and Cohesion

Once conflict erupts, it undermines interpersonal and communal trust, destroys the norms and values that underpin cooperation and collective action, and diminishes the capacity of communities to manage conflict through nonviolent means. One of the legacies of protracted civil strife—in addition to the destruction of physical and human capital—has been the displacement of millions of people. The displacement process in particular disrupts the underpinnings of social capital by removing men and women from their traditional socioeconomic environment, patterns of social organization, and collective action and eroding the foundations of previous forms of leadership and accountability (Holtzman and Nezam 2004). Once the conflict ends, even if other forms of capital are replenished, sustainable economic and social development will be constrained unless positive social capital can also be rebuilt (Colletta and Cullen 2000).

Rebuilding social capital involves revitalizing civil society and its capacity for collective action, through the promotion of local associations, community participation, and accountability. When it comes to reintegration and post-conflict reconstruction, donor agencies have a role to play beyond promoting employment and training for ex-combatants or rebuilding infrastructure and services. Development actors in general, but particularly those working in societies emerging from conflict, need to help to reweave the torn social fabric and support positive social capital by nurturing institutions and processes that can strengthen social cohesion and inclusion, manage diversity, prevent a return to violent conflict, and sustain peace and reconciliation efforts (adapted from Colletta and Cullen 2000). Without a reweaving of the social fabric and greater social cohesion, post-conflict societies will find it difficult to sustain development efforts and will remain vulnerable to the reemergence of conflict. Clearly, the rebuilding of social capital and social cohesion are deeply gendered processes, even though they are still generally described in a nongendered manner.

Development Dynamics: Empowering Communities and Promoting Social Cohesion through CDD

Development efforts in post-conflict settings need to focus on regenerating social capital and inclusion to build the basis for sustainable peace and effective longer-term development. Development approaches in many agencies, including the World Bank, increasingly emphasize participatory and CDD processes to help strengthen social cohesion within and possibly between communities (linking social capital). By linking participatory development approaches with financing mechanisms that explicitly respond to community demands, CDD aims to empower local communities by placing the control of decisions, resources, and accountability at beneficiary level. Community decisionmaking, project planning, implementation, and monitoring thus have the potential not only to meet the needs of rebuilding social and economic infrastructure, but also to start the process of rebuilding positive social capital. Because of its potential to rebuild relations of trust and greater social inclusion, CDD approaches can facilitate reconciliation and the integration of refugees, former combatants, and internally displaced persons. An important assumption underpinning this approach in a post-conflict environment is that it can contribute to greater social cohesion and mutual trust, including the possibility (as yet untested) that more empowered communities, with a higher stock of social capital, are better able to manage conflict without resorting to violence.[53]

The adoption of CDD approaches in post-conflict reconstruction can encourage more gender-balanced representation in local decisionmaking processes and, if sustained, provide a springboard for greater women's empowerment and involvement in broader decisionmaking and political processes. But these complex processes require careful contextualization and adaptation in each setting (see box 9.1).

Development Challenges: Addressing Constraints on Women's Participation

CDD approaches generally pay particular attention to women's participation and representation in decisionmaking structures (e.g., village development councils) and processes (e.g., community meetings to select subprojects). Although not always explicitly taken into account in project design, many factors discourage and constrain women's participation, including:

- In most traditional societies, men are expected to represent and speak on behalf of their household and village within the community and to the outside world; in some cases, such as in Timor-Leste, even when there is a rule requiring 50/50 gender representation in village development councils, it is reported that a

---

Box 9.1 CDD in the West Bank and Gaza
          Embraces Women

CDD was introduced in the West Bank and Gaza portfolio initially
through the Holst Employment Generation Program and later through
the Bank-funded Community Development Projects. Most assistance
initially concentrated on large urban development projects where community participation and, in particular, women's participation was non-
existent, either in decisionmaking or implementation. Men who had lost
their jobs in Israel were the initial target population for the public works
programs. Beneficiary assessments conducted to evaluate the programs
showed that the targeted beneficiaries were not necessarily the most in
need and a population segment, which included women-headed households, had been completely ignored. Similarly, monitoring and evaluation of the first Community Development Project showed that a large
number of proposed projects were in the road sector. It was also noted
that women were rarely consulted in the decisionmaking phase or in
implementation. Further analysis through women-only meetings revealed that, while women prioritized projects in the social sectors—
health and education for their children—men tended to focus on economic infrastructure, mainly roads, and used the cultural taboos/
conflict environment as an excuse to ignore the views of the other half
of the population.

The next project required that communities include women members
in the local project committees and that implementing agencies hire
women community development managers to monitor and further encourage women participation. Gender participation is not a given, it
needs nurturing through a sustained and supportive process and should
not be introduced too quickly so as not to disrupt cultural sensitivities
(Meenakshi 2003).

---

woman council member's husband often represents her (see
box 9.2). In the first Kecamatan Development Project (KDP) in
Indonesia, when the project mandated that two out of five village
representatives had to be women, the village head (*Kades*) simply
appointed the women representatives without consultation
(World Bank Jakarta/PPK 2003).

• Women are expected not to voice their opinion when the men are
making decisions, a perception often shared by men and
women—although in Timor-Leste women complained that they
are not given a chance to participate because men dominate the
meetings (Ostergaard 2003).

Box 9.2 Women Gain Equal Representation on Local
          Councils in Timor-Leste

In the World Bank–funded East Timor Community Empowerment Project, equal representation of women and men on the councils was supported by the women's arm of the National Council of Timorese Resistance, which was also represented at the village level. This was quite a radical experiment in a very traditional society with high illiteracy. The equal representation requirement was interpreted at the hamlet and village levels to mean that women represent the women of the hamlet and men represent the men. In a recent independent evaluation of the project's three funding cycles, the list of council members that the project management unit provided showed 100 percent compliance with the 50/50 representation rule. Interviews with village and subdistrict council leaders confirmed that most, but not all, councils had an equal number of men and women. A survey of 328 of the first councils elected in 2000, however, showed that only two had appointed women as council leaders. Moreover, the number of active council members has been declining, and women's participation has decreased more than that of men. It is frequently reported that a woman council member's husband represents her, de facto replacing her on the council (Ostergaard 2003).

- Women shoulder a heavy domestic burden, especially taking care of children, and this burden may be especially high after conflict as women head more households. As with female ex-combatants, women-headed households and widows tend to become invisible in post-conflict reconstruction (UNDESA 2001). In Indonesia women cannot legally be considered head of a household and, in some areas, the very term female-head is resisted. Widows often face even more serious ostracism and isolation, and even danger—in Aceh, women avoid admitting that they are widows since the military assumes that the deceased husband must have died fighting for the rebel movement.[54]
- A sense of inferiority and lack of confidence—often the result of illiteracy, class, or lineage distinctions—makes women reluctant to participate. In Subang, Indonesia, one woman from the village of Pakuhaji repeatedly referred to herself as *Saya cumin orang kecil* (I am just a little person). By not attending these meetings, the villagers, convinced that they have nothing to offer, avoid the possibility of being embarrassed in public for their illiteracy. The poorer members especially feel intimidated by the other villagers (Wong 2002). In Sierra Leone, Richards et al. (2004) point out

that women from powerful lineages are more likely to participate and speak up than women from weak lineages or unmarried
women—women from powerful lineages are likely to act in the
interest of their lineage rather than of their gender.

- Logistics can be a binding constraint. Women often have to
travel long distances just to attend a meeting, which is often
made worse by physical damage and neglect of infrastructure in
post-conflict settings. In West Sumatra, women living in remote
areas must travel hours, often by foot and over difficult conditions, to attend a village development committee meeting. If the
meeting is held in the morning, they must start very early, and if
it is held later in the afternoon, they must make their way home
in the dark (Limura and Kawamo 2003). In Timor-Leste, women
often cannot travel unaccompanied or with a male who is not
their husband, which limits their ability to participate in subdistrict development council meetings (Ostergaard 2003).

- The opportunity cost of attending meetings can be high too, especially for the poor. In Subang, Indonesia, a poor villager makes
Rp 5,000 (about $0.6) per day and what they earn that day may
be what they eat. By attending a meeting, poor villagers are possibly losing their meal for that day (Limura and Kawamo 2003). For
poor women, the financial cost is on top of their household duties.

Policy Options

Bearing in mind that, as noted above, there is a need for additional
research and analysis to draw more systematic policy recommendations, a number of lessons and approaches are emerging on ways to
improve both the level and effectiveness of women's participation in
community-driven processes. A key emerging lesson is that mandating
50/50 gender representation in village and community committees and
councils, while an important first step, is not enough and is often not
sustained. Moreover, attending a meeting is not the same as actively
participating. Experience with the first phase of the Indonesia KDP
showed that even when women did attend, they would not always actively convey their ideas, defend their proposals, decide on proposal
rankings and funding, or participate in the implementation and monitoring of the activities funded. Ensuring women's active participation
in community processes requires additional efforts, which in turn need
to be evaluated in each setting and cultural context. Options include:

- *Adopting CDD approaches.* CDD approaches provide an opportunity for local women to take part in decisionmaking on the

design, implementation, and monitoring of reconstruction assistance. The gender aspects of CDD approaches in reconstruction need to be further analyzed, while the gendered effects on individual projects or programs need to be monitored and evaluated to provide feedback for future project design.

- *Mobilizing the support of men and the community as a whole to support women's participation.* An emerging lesson suggests that women's participation is both more feasible and effective when men are supportive (e.g., Wong 2002). More broadly, this suggests developing a community consensus on the need for and the design of mechanisms to strengthen women's participation in community development processes. A rights-based approach that does not overtly challenge prevailing social norms and that can demonstrate communitywide benefits from greater women's participation may be a good starting point. If combined with careful community sensitization and socialization efforts, it may stand a better chance of generating support for women's participation than merely mandating more equal gender representation.

- *Investing in training community and council leaders.* Another critical factor in sustaining women's participation appears to be the council leaders' leadership abilities. The Timor-Leste evaluation noted that investing in training village council leaders, including on gender aspects, would have likely produced higher returns in terms of increased and sustained participation (Ostergaard 2003).

- *Investing in local gender facilitators.* Experiences from Timor-Leste and Indonesia suggest that CDD facilitators play a key role. The KDP gender evaluation (Wong 2002) noted the need for more female facilitators and pointed to consistent reports that women feel more comfortable speaking freely if there is a female facilitator. Female facilitators can also represent an important role model for women in villages, especially if they are locally recruited rather than drawn from national or international NGOs, which often have no or few roots in the local community.[55] In addition to trying to recruit more female facilitators, there is need to invest in gender training for both male and female facilitators.

- *Adapting the timing of meetings to women's needs and time constraints.* In Sierra Leone, Richards et al. (2004) point out that female elders and young nursing mothers favor different times of day to attend meetings. It is almost impossible for young women, especially those from weak lineages, to attend meetings outside the village at any time, but especially during the farming season. In Indonesia, if the meeting is set during market days or holy *adat* days, women will not attend (World Bank Jakarta/PPK 2003). In KDP, meetings often follow right after religious gatherings—combining the two back-to-back but not mixing the contents spares women the extra time and transportation costs (Wong 2002).

- *Considering providing or facilitating transport to attend meetings.* Easing the transportation burden can reduce women's time, risk, and opportunity cost of attending meetings outside the village. This can be done either by organizing pickup services or through a transportation subsidy.
- *Organizing separate women's meetings to prepare for presentations to wider community or council meetings.* Projects in Timor-Leste and Indonesia have found it effective to organize meetings of women representatives before council meetings to enable them to prepare their cases and formulate joint proposals. Helping women to prepare before important meetings appears to strengthen their self-confidence, enable them to be more prepared to argue for their proposals or priorities, and improve the prospect that they will participate more actively in community decisionmaking processes (Wong 2002; Ostergaard 2003).
- *Encouraging innovation and experimentation.* An interesting KDP approach has been to encourage each district KDP team to compete over who has the best idea for increasing women's participation. The 25 winners are rewarded with a write-up in the national newsletter, a $60 prize, and an entry into the operational manual. This small innovation is reportedly generating considerable local thinking and pilots.[56]
- *Developing a strong gender monitoring and evaluation component as integral part of project design.* In the case of Timor-Leste, no effort was made to develop gender-disaggregated project monitoring data, which makes it difficult to evaluate and address gender-related issues (Ostergaard 2003).

A number of additional points are worth noting. First, as emphasized by Richards et al. (2004), it is important not to waste the limited amount of time that women have available to attend meetings, even when additional support is provided, in badly or incompetently designed meetings. Perhaps more than any other single factor, this is likely to quickly discourage women from making time available to attend meetings. If it is to lead to women's empowerment, participation needs to be for a purpose, not for its own sake.

Second, there is a need to evaluate the issue of women's participation in CDD approaches within a broader and more contextualized social analysis. Richards et al. (2004) point out that CDD approaches assume too easily that women's vulnerability can be addressed simply by targeting benefits to women and having women representation in committees or councils. Striving for women's participation without an understanding of the social context may not produce the intended results and risks consolidating existing patterns of exclusion and disempowerment. In parts of Sierra Leone, for example, it matters a great deal whether a woman member of a village development council is a wife from a weak lineage or a member of the elite (e.g., the wife or sister of a paramount chief). The latter is likely to act in the interest of her lineage and elite alliances rather than in response to gender concerns or broad appeals to gender solidarity. Thus, apparently successful examples of gender empowerment and voice may mask more complex cleavages based on class, lineages, religion, or ethnicity. The authors decry the lack of donor and NGO social analysis in the communities they assist, under the tyranny of project deadlines, disbursement targets, and reporting requirements.[57]

Third, CDD approaches in post-conflict settings pose a particularly difficult dilemma in terms of the trade-off between trying to respond quickly to meet the urgent needs of war-torn communities versus the more painstaking and lengthier efforts required to better understand the social context where community development is being encouraged and getting the participatory processes right—often referred to as the CDD project's socialization phase. In nonconflict settings, CDD projects include a relatively long (often over six months) community planning period to foster strong and active participation in setting priorities and making decisions (Cliffe et al. 2003). Where there are strong cultural barriers to women's participation, the socialization and participatory planning process is not only more critical, but also likely to be more complex and lengthy. In Indonesia, the KDP socialization phase to support women's participation is reported to have taken up to 18 months, requiring intensive facilitation of women-only groups, training, and gradual scaling up into larger groups until women felt capable of actively participating in traditionally male-dominated community meetings.[58] This presents a particular challenge in post-conflict settings where there is great pressure to disburse funds to communities affected by the violence and often little patience—by donor agencies and client governments—with lengthy socialization and preparatory processes that do not appear to show immediate results and benefits.

Fourth, introducing formal gender participation requirements or quotas—such as the 50/50 rule or earmarked funding for women's projects—runs the risk of generating a community backlash. Some preliminary indications emerging from Timor-Leste and Indonesia suggest that this may be more in response to the perception that these affirmative action measures are externally imposed rather than due solely to resistance from men who feel threatened by a weakening of their power or the undermining of traditional norms and social values. In Timor-Leste, as long as men and women selected the women candidates to a council, there seemed to be little resistance. In Indonesia's KDP, several *kecamatans* passed their own regulations requiring that a meeting be cancelled if there is not a minimum level of women's participation (generally 30 percent). This suggests that while gender-balanced representation may be useful and necessary initially, quotas may be divisive.[59] More effective and sustainable participation is likely to emerge only when the community as a whole validates and supports the need for women's participation.

Fifth, much of the experience with CDD and women's participation in conflict settings is anecdotal and not as yet systematized. Although there is a growing body of work on engendering participation and empowerment in development activities more generally, there is little systematic analysis and documentation of experiences in conflict-affected countries. There has been little effort to develop an evaluation framework and to benchmark these processes. As a result, to enhance women's participation in a post-conflict setting, each new CDD process is forced to reinvent the wheel. Moreover, without such a systematic evaluation and conceptual framework, it becomes difficult to argue the case that if women's participation is to become meaningful, CDD processes and the project funding mechanisms that seek to support them must be applied more flexibly and become more responsive to the complexities involved.

CHAPTER 10

Policy Options

Overview

POLICY OPTIONS PRIMARILY RELATE to the Bank's mandate and agenda, but may be applied by other agencies working in the post-conflict reconstruction and development nexus. The policies focus on longer-term development challenges instead of short-term humanitarian relief, and they explicitly go beyond the notion of women and men only as conflict victims. Although the policy options fall broadly within the World Bank's mandate, it does not imply that the Bank will have a comparative advantage relative to other actors that are active in post-conflict. Even when the Bank is not directly involved, it often plays a key role in post-conflict reconstruction and thus the policy options need to inform its broader development and donor coordination efforts. Conflict has complex and often contradictory effects on gender relations, especially in terms of women's empowerment and/or disempowerment. Policy options are offered to try to ensure and sustain more balanced gender relations in conflict-affected societies. However, there is no substitute for context-specific analysis—for an assessment of reality on the ground and the country-specific scope for policy reforms and options.

To enhance the implementation of the suggested policy options, a number of intra-organizational requirements are outlined that an institution such as the World Bank should consider. They relate to the need to develop concrete gender and armed conflict policies, to translate these policies into action plans and benchmarks, to monitor and evaluate gender- and conflict-related activities to assess their impact on gender roles and relationships in conflict, to sensitize and train staff, and to incorporate gender and conflict issues into existing programs, projects, tools, and instruments. Finally, four other relevant issues are discussed: objectives to be set, timing of interventions, interventions' target group, and other challenges to be considered.

Relevance

Table 10.1, below, summarizes the policy options discussed in this review. A number of points are worth noting.

1. The policy options are broadly in line with the Bank's conflict and development mandate. Although some recommendations (e.g., gender and formal peace processes or women's participation in formal and informal political processes) may seem to relate to peacemaking activities or political activities beyond the Bank's mandate, the authors have approached these issues from the perspectives of governance, participation, and voice, which are consistent with the Bank's approach and mandate.
2. Policy options focus on the conflict and development nexus; they emphasize the longer-term development challenges rather than shorter-term needs, which relate more to humanitarian relief.
3. The policy options go beyond the notion of women and men as only conflict survivors and attempt to provide options regarding the multifaceted, often different and complex roles that women and men play in conflict.
4. The policy options attempt to capitalize on the positive gender role changes during conflict to support more equal gender relations during post-conflict reconstruction and longer-term development processes, as well as to mitigate possible negative impacts.
5. Although policy options fall broadly within the Bank's mandate, operations, and experiences, it does not imply that the Bank will have a comparative advantage relative to other actors in the field or that it will take the lead in all these areas. Even when the Bank is not directly involved, it is critical to be well versed in the issues and approaches of other actors to ensure stronger donor coordination and informed dialogue with government counterparts, especially in post-conflict reconstruction programs and strategies.

Capitalizing on Empowering Gender Role Changes

This study has highlighted conflict's varied and complex impact on gender roles and relationships. To mitigate negative impacts and to take advantage of positive gender changes, the reality on the ground must be ascertained and the actual scope assessed to implement policy measures. Discussed below are a number of factors that need to be considered in assessing the scope for action.

Table 10.1 Policy Options

Disarmament, Demobilization, and Reintegration	1. Target all women and men in (ir)regular armies with post-conflict assistance: • *Recast the definition of female combatants;* • *Track and identify female and male ex-combatants well in advance of the DDR program;* • *Consider targeting female dependents of ex-combatants in their own right and separating them from their male counterparts; and* • *Use women-favored communication channels to disseminate information on upcoming DDR programs.* 2. Gender-sensitize demobilization activities and facilities: • *Support new forms of social organization for women and men that return home; and* • *Consider potential gender differences in encampment facilities, predischarge information, and other relevant areas.* 3. Anticipate male and female soldiers' different economic, social, and psychological reintegration: • *(Economic) Consider female soldiers' limited access to land, relatively few skills, restricted mobility, and the strict labor divisions that they may face;* • *(Social) Prepare communities for male and female soldiers' return;* • *(Social) Assist female soldiers in dealing with the often unequal gender relations at home compared to the army;* • *(Social) Combat negative stigmatization of female soldiers and soldiers' wives;* • *(Social) Establish separate veterans' groups for male and female soldiers;* • *(Social) Rely on and support existing informal community efforts, that are often women-led, to support social reintegration; and* • *(Psychological) Ensure the presence of female counselors who know how to work with GBV survivors.*
Gender-Based and Sexual Violence	4. Raise GBV awareness, involving both women and men.

(*continued on next page*)

Table 10.1 (Continued)

	5. Provide psychological assistance to all actors involved in GBV: • *Support local counseling capacities, including both female and male counselors; and* • *Where possible, adopt local counseling techniques, while ensuring that female counselors are present and that local counseling techniques are women-friendly.* 6. Incorporate support to GBV survivors in medical assistance programs. 7. Build the institutional capacity of actors involved (such as the police, judiciary, and border patrols): • *Involve women's organizations in GBV training; and* • *Establish special GBV units within the police and other relevant institutions.* 8. Consider providing assistance to male GBV survivors.
Formal Peace Processes	9. Encourage the incorporation of gender issues into peace accords and political rehabilitation activities: • *Provide gender awareness training to women and men in office; and* • *Develop wider processes of political consultation and representation such as women's organizations.* 10. Support women's and men's equal participation in decisionmaking structures and elections: • *Train and recruit women and men to stand as political candidates at all levels;* • *Foster discussion about women's and men's political participation;* • *Carefully use quotas and other affirmative action to increase the number of women in politics; and* • *Assess impact of a more gender-balanced political participation.*
Informal Peace Processes and Rebuilding Civil Society	11. Strengthen women's organizations and other CSOs to bridge the gap between informal and formal peace processes: • *Provide capacity building and training to women's organizations;* • *Support women's organizations to increase their visibility and exposure;* • *Encourage interaction between women's organizations and actors in formal peace processes; and*

Table 10.1 (Continued)

	• *Support female civil society leaders to enter formal politics.*
	12. Assist women's organizations and other CSOs during and after conflict and consider them as the foundation for a post-conflict civil society: • *Ensure long-term support to women's organizations;* • *Promote the organizational skills of women's CSOs;* • *Integrate women and women's organizations in longer-term rehabilitation and development efforts; and* • *Improve donor coordination within a longer-term strategy.*
Legal Framework	13. Increase commitment to existing international legislation.
	14. Gender-sensitize the constitution and other laws at the national level: • *Ensure women's and men's involvement in drafting new legislation;* • *Inform and train women and men on their legal rights; and* • *Encourage the judiciary to enforce gender-sensitive laws.*
	15. Provide for the establishment of national machinery for gender equality.
	16. Encourage judicial mechanisms to acknowledge, condemn, and prosecute all crimes against women and men in conflict situations.
	17. Facilitate the process of survivors and witnesses sharing and reporting experiences.
Work (General)	18. Ease household burdens that may limit participation outside the home.
	19. Anticipate women's parenting tasks.
	20. Target women and men equally without reinforcing gender-stereotypical labor divisions.
	21. Develop a long-term, integrated approach toward gender and employment.
Agricultural Work	22. Short-term: provide women and men with the means to survive.
	23. Medium and longer-term: ensure equal access to land and other productive assets.
	24. Gender-sensitize agricultural support services.
	25. Revive self-help groups, often including women's CSOs.
Informal Urban Work	26. Deal critically with microcredit programs.

(*continued on next page*)

Table 10.1 (Continued)

	27. Set up vocational training programs on the basis of a proper market research and gender analysis.
	28. Stimulate the improvement of labor conditions and rights.
Formal Urban Work	29. Encourage women's employment in "traditional" women's sectors.
	30. Certify women's and men's newly acquired skills and experiences.
	31. Undertake positive action to involve women in rehabilitation and development activities.
	32. Improve basic employment conditions for women and men.
Rehabilitating Social Services	33. Restart public education and health services: • *Value professionally women's/men's efforts in education and health;* • *Take community-based or home-based education and health systems as a starting point for rehabilitating the education and health sectors; and* • *Employ women and men in reconstruction efforts.*
	34. Gender-sensitize health and education services: • *Broaden the focus beyond primary education;* • *Encourage everyone (women, men, boys, and girls) to participate in education;* • *Prioritize rural girls' education; and* • *Develop gender-balanced education systems and training.*
Community-Driven Development	35. Increase women's participation and empowerment in CDD projects. • *Adopt CDD approaches in post-conflict reconstruction, while mobilizing the support of men and communities for women's participation;* • *Invest in (gender) training community leaders and local gender facilitators;* • *Adapt timing of community meetings to meet women's needs and time constraints and consider facilitating transport so more women can attend meetings;* • *Organize separate women's meetings to help them prepare for presentations to the wider community or council meetings;* • *Encourage local innovation and experimentation on ways to improve women's participation; and* • *Develop strong gender monitoring and evaluation components in project design.*

Given that a conflict's overall impact is overwhelmingly negative and traumatic for those involved, certain gender role changes that result from conflict clearly have a *disempowering effect* on women, for instance, the substantial burden imposed on women due to the breakdown in health and education services.

However, certain gender role changes can also have an *empowering* effect on women. This is especially the case when women gain access to new employment opportunities, but here too there are complex effects—some women will see the new opportunities as an escape from prevailing labor constraints, while others may consider it more a matter of survival. Similarly, female soldiers may encounter more equal gender relations in armed forces, but they may also face exploitative relationships while being a soldier. Each situation is different and requires contextual analysis to determine whether the changes are positive or negative and thus whether they should be supported or attempts made to correct them in post-conflict reconstruction.

Due to a lack of data, it is not clear whether *potentially empowering* gender role changes that benefit women actually take place during conflict or can be sustained. This is particularly true for women's participation in formal and informal peace processes during conflict, as well as their increased participation in the formal labor force after conflict.

The *empowering effect of gender role changes must not be overestimated*. Women's and men's roles and relations in conflict are usually closely related to those during peacetime, which may explain why the normalization of post-conflict life is often characterized by a reintroduction of gender roles and relations from the pre-conflict period. Conflict may well create space for a temporary redefinition of gender relations, but it often does not change them fundamentally (UN 2002). Gender role changes often lead to limited increases in women's decisionmaking powers and political participation after conflict, but the ideological bases underpinning gender relations appear to remain largely unchanged or are reinforced quickly after conflict (El-Bushra et al. 2002; Meintjes et al. 2001). Gender relations can become polarized during conflict, and prevalent stereotypes of gender-appropriate behavior may be more strictly enforced after conflict (Farr 2002). In addition, *de facto* gains are often not translated into *de jure* changes in women's status—they have the responsibilities but not the power (El-Bushra et al. 2002). These conditions suggest the need to adopt a longer-term perspective in supporting measures to empower women and seek greater gender balance in development efforts.

External support may be key to sustaining positive gender roles in conflict settings. Whereas some authors caution that addressing gender equity in unstable post-conflict environments is likely to be an exercise in futility (e.g., Strickland and Duvvury 2003) or counterproductive, the authors of this review believe that the international community can and should support the empowering effects of gender role changes. More equal gender relations need to form an integral part of international efforts to rebuild the economic and social fabric of war-torn societies. Clearly, the nature and extent of external support needs to be country-specific and based on a good local understanding of changes in gender roles. External support must also assess the cultural and social contexts and local demand and support for such transformation. Without a minimum, critical level of domestic support, it is unlikely that externally driven change will be effective or sustainable.[60] It is also critical to ascertain consistency with local women's and men's own agendas, because without their participation, sustainable change in gender relations will not be possible.

Intra-Organizational Requirements

On a practical level, to implement the suggested policy options the Bank may need to consider its own organizational structure as well. Bouta and Frerks' earlier work (2002, 2003) on 16 international organizations working in conflict-affected countries shows what kind of intra-organizational requirements are needed to better address women's and men's roles. The Bank can build on some of these lessons and best practices, as follows:

1. Gather additional information on women's and men's specific roles in each conflict situation.
2. Set specific organizational objectives and develop concrete guidelines, action plans, and benchmarks to address women's and men's roles in conflict and translate existing policies into practice. Lack of specificity usually complicates the implementation of gender-related activities. Practical guidelines and toolkits would be helpful in mainstreaming gender in conflict-affected countries. While these tools exist or are being developed for stable countries, as seen in this review, conflict-affected countries present a more complex set of gender issues that would justify the development of guidelines and tools that specifically focus on conflict.
3. Carefully monitor and evaluate gender-related activities and their outputs to assess whether and how these have affected women's and men's roles in conflict. So far there have been few policy evaluations. There remain numerous uncertainties on the impact of gender-related instruments and approaches.

4. Increase attention for and commitment to gender roles in conflict among staff at all organizational levels, especially for staff working in conflict-affected areas. A suggestion may be to include gender and conflict as criteria in staff recruitment, appraisal, and training.

5. Attempt to involve local women and men equally in the preparation, implementation, monitoring, and evaluation of gender-related activities. While this obviously will not guarantee that gender is taken into account, it may well increase the chances of it being considered.

6. Enhance expertise on gender and conflict by providing staff training at the Bank and to local women's and men's organizations. Training could be adapted to the organization's specific mandate and activities, to the specific conflict situation, and to the specific roles, vulnerabilities, and skills of the local women and men to be addressed in the field.

7. Attempt to incorporate gender and conflict issues increasingly into the organization's activities, instruments, and tools, such as post-conflict needs assessments, poverty assessments, CDD approaches, Country Assistance and Transitional Support Strategies, and Poverty Reduction Strategy processes.

8. Increasingly link the topics of gender, conflict, and development cooperation and bring corresponding expertise and information together.

Although the Bank has well-developed gender and development policies and operational procedures, the conflict and development nexus is still being explored. As in the case of gender per se, this requires mainstreaming a conflict lens and conflict-sensitizing regular activities: "It should be realized that simply entering conflict areas with 'traditional' development assistance is not appropriate and that adaptations in programming are often a condition for sustainable results. Development activities need to be adapted and sensitized to respond to the challenge of conflict" (Bouta and Frerks 2001). Likewise, the gender and conflict link is not yet fully articulated in the Bank's work and needs further conceptualization and operational guidance. Some useful experiences have been gained through the implementation of innovative programs targeted on gender aspects of conflict, but it is necessary to digest and learn from these experiences.

The overall challenge is to arrive at a comprehensive understanding of gender roles, relations, and dynamics in all conflict phases. This underlines the Bank's efforts to move from a "survivor discourse" about women in conflict and a largely post-conflict reconstruction perspective, to a broader agenda encompassing the different conflict phases and the Bank's different strategies and activities. As in most other agencies in this field, the Bank's gender and conflict agendas need to be linked conceptually, analytically, institutionally, and in procedural and operational terms (Bouta and Frerks 2002). Since gender and conflict are crosscutting themes, gender and conflict sensitivity need to be achieved concurrently and on the basis of an understanding of their mutual and dynamic interrelationship.

Objectives, Timing, Target Groups, and Dilemmas

In addition to these organizational considerations, the Bank may also need to consider the objectives, timing, target groups, and challenges that its interventions pose. These issues are briefly discussed below.

Regarding *objectives,* on the one hand, the Bank should focus on changing gender roles in conflict and, on the other hand, concentrate on helping to transform gender relations and ideologies in conflict-affected countries. As observed above, these are not necessarily related. Concerning the first, the key objective would be to capitalize on positive gender role changes. At a minimum, the Bank could support women and men to sustain the roles, positions, skills, and opportunities gained during conflict in the post-conflict phase. The transformation of gender relations is a difficult, long-term process during peace and in conflict situations. It is not just about implementing targeted activities, but also requires interventions that touch on the underlying norms and values that define gender relations and power dynamics (Strickland and Duvvury 2003). Information and sensitization campaigns on women's and men's equal rights could form part of such creative interventions. The long-term objective should contribute to more equal gender relations in the post-conflict phase. However, some modesty is called for as such changes depend largely on each society's internal dynamics.

For gender-related interventions in conflict-affected countries, *timing* is crucial. As observed throughout this review, the transition phase from war to peace offers the best moment to sustain gender role changes and to lay the basis for future gender relations. It is here, when women and men have not yet returned to stability, that gender relations are still in the process of being redefined, and women's organizations have not yet split up or been weakened. Despite the fact that transition phases may be hard to define and may differ from context to context, the Bank should get an early start. This could be explicitly addressed in its preparatory analytical work, its Watching Briefs, and its Transitional Support Strategies. It is also essential that gender be fully and comprehensively addressed as a crosscutting theme in post-conflict needs assessments, as these often become the reconstruction roadmaps.

There is no blueprint for choosing the *target group* for gender-related interventions in conflict. Agencies have adopted various approaches for including women and men in their conflict-related activities. Some have opted for an exclusive approach that only focuses on certain vulnerable groups of women, such as widows and female-headed households. Others have provided assistance to all women, not exclusively to vulnerable women. Particularly with regard to equal rights issues such as access to land and property, agencies generally agree on the need to promote all women's rights instead of only the rights of specific vulnerable groups of women (Kumar 2001; ICRC 2001). Again, other agencies have favored an inclusive community-based approach, as segregating women and men in crisis settings can reinforce perceptions of women's vulnerability and create gender conflict and competition (UNCHS 1999; ILO 2001). Moreover, providing community resources may also present opportunities to initiate a process of rebuilding trust and reciprocity. These various approaches are combined in many community-driven projects, including some that are Bank-supported. They provide assistance to the community as a whole, but ensure women's active involvement through actions such as quotas or requiring that proposed subprojects also cover women's needs. Regardless of the approach chosen, from a longer-term development perspective, it will be impossible to sustain changing gender roles and support more equal gender relations without effectively targeting both women and men.

Finally, irrespective of approaches and organizational choices, the gender-specific roles and dynamics during and after conflict involve a number of difficult *challenges,* including:

- How to demobilize and reintegrate female and male soldiers, including those in support roles, in their own right and without creating the impression that they receive preferential treatment compared to the civilian population—i.e., that violence is rewarded;
- How to balance the contradictory aspects of survivor and victim, of empowerment and vulnerability, and of dependent aid versus independent change to capitalize on emerging windows of opportunity;
- How to reconcile the need for speed in post-conflict settings with the greater time required to engender rehabilitation programs;

- How to relate donor-supported gender agendas and women's needs to local cultures and practices, avoiding the perception that they are externally imposed; and
- How to support affirmative action without generating negative side effects or backlashes.

There are no definite answers to these questions and all agencies must struggle with them but, as this review has tried to show and document, there are relevant lessons and best practices that can offer guidance. Each agency must assess these issues in its specific context and determine their applicability.

CHAPTER II

Further Analysis on Gender, Conflict, and Development

Overview

DESPITE INCREASED ATTENTION to the interrelationship among gender, conflict, and development, a number of key areas need further analysis and research. First, there is a need for a more comprehensive gender focus beyond reductionist perspectives on women's roles. Second, conflict analysis and early-warning indicators need to be engendered—most analytical and policy models, approaches, tools, instruments, and conflict checklists lack a gender-specific theoretical and operational basis.

Other areas that call for greater analysis include the following:

1. Certain gender role changes need further analysis, as described in this study. For instance, regarding gender and formal peace processes, there is very limited information on gender and conflict prevention. The role of men and men's CSOs in informal peace processes is also underresearched.
2. Discussions on (militarized) masculinity and femininity need to be further related to women's and men's positions in conflict to better understand if and how conflict can lead to more balanced gender relations.
3. The subject of male identities, the link between masculinity and violence, the need to encourage a nonmilitarized masculinity, and the particular position of adolescents and young men are underexposed areas in the literature. Although there is anthropological work on these issues, few if any studies were prepared with a policy focus for development agencies.
4. Although there has been considerable attention on child soldiers, there appears to be little gendered analysis of issues affecting child soldiers, especially in terms of psychosocial needs and post-conflict mental trauma.

5. Future studies, particularly field case studies, should examine gender's relative importance compared with other identity markers in shaping women's and men's roles and relationships in conflict-affected areas.

6. An important underresearched topic, especially in terms of case studies and policy recommendations, is how to engender post-conflict macroeconomic policies and state and institution building.

7. There is a risk that the interrelationship of gender, conflict, and development will become a separate research topic in itself. It would be more useful, however, if studies capitalized on existing insights in the gender, conflict, and development cooperation fields. Future studies may well combine information available in these three fields to come to a more informed analysis on the interrelationship between gender, conflict, and development.

8. Analyses of social capital and cohesion and their importance in post-conflict reconstruction explore various cleavages within society, but remarkably little attention has been paid to their gender dimension. How do gender roles undermine social cohesion, and how can gender roles be harnessed to promote social cohesion?

9. Policymakers and practitioners, in particular, and academicians should pay more attention to the need for overall transformative approaches that can fundamentally alter the balance of power in gender relations as post-conflict societies rebuild.

Specific Gender Roles

Taking the gender roles described in this report as a reference point, the role of ex-soldiers is the first area needing further analysis. From a preventive viewpoint, studies should focus on how to find alternatives to the option of (re)joining (ir)regular armies before and during conflict. Additional analysis should determine how to provide women and men with income, social status, power, recognition, and enhanced feelings of manhood or womanhood outside of joining fighting forces.[61] The gender and disarmament issue also needs further analysis. Although often mentioned as part of gender-sensitizing DDR programs, it has received much less attention than demobilization and particularly reintegration (Strickland and Duvvury 2003). On the reintegration of female and male ex-soldiers, extra attention is required on how to target assistance not only to female combatants, but also to soldiers' wives, abducted women acting as sex slaves, and women in host communities.[62]

With regard to gender and formal peace processes, the potential impact of gender perspectives on conflict prevention and preventive diplomacy remains seriously underresearched (UN 2002). Despite the fact that various authors stress the importance of conducting gender-sensitive conflict prevention planning through gender-specific risk and impact assessment (Sikoska and Solomon 2002), hardly any work has been done on this issue. One exception may be the Schmeidl and Piza-Lopez (2002) attempt to gender-sensitize early warning mechanisms. According to them, gender-sensitizing such mechanisms means incorporating indicators that capture gender-related changes in society over time in data gathering and analysis. It also means integrating gender analysis and perspectives into the formulation of response options, which should ensure that discriminatory policies are not perpetuated in post-conflict situations or newfound freedoms reversed. In this connection, they argue that with women's active participation, early-warning systems can better use the untapped potential of women's networks and organizations. The increased involvement of women's groups also facilitates potential conflict responses at a political and humanitarian level to address the specific vulnerabilities of women and men alike. However, Schmeidl and Pisa-Lopez admit that their work is only a first proposal, so more systematic and usable information about women and men in pre-conflict phases needs to be collected to turn gender perspectives into concrete early-warning indicators (Rehn and Sirleaf 2002).

More research is also needed on women's formal political participation *during* conflict. It is not clear whether gender role changes really increase women's participation in formal political processes and high-level positions. There is also lack of information and analysis on the role of men and men's organizations in informal peace processes.

Finally, more study is required concerning gender and formal urban employment. There is a need to better understand whether women's participation *during* conflict increases because of loosening labor relations or decreases because of a likely reduction in formal employment. Additional research is needed on the factors that affect women's participation in formal employment *after* conflict. The literature reviewed mentions the importance of enhancing women's access to formal employment, but offers few lessons, best practices, and concrete policy options. The debate on "economies of war" has not yet been scrutinized from a gender perspective, nor has the extent to which women are involved in and benefit from such economies. In most conflict-affected countries, war economies may generate incomes for a substantial number of women and men, but a gender analysis is lacking.

Masculinity, Femininity, and Gender Relations

Masculinity and femininity need to be further related to women's and men's positions in conflict. Masculinities and femininities are negotiated interpretations of what it means to be a man or a woman. Conflict situations seem to create a rather militarized masculinity, which is deeply oppressive of women and also of many men. It exaggerates gender difference and inequality and dictates complementary worlds for men and women, during and after conflict. Although the women's and men's positions that masculinities and femininities generate are never fully determinant of reality, and never altogether erase individual agency (Cockburn and Zarkov 2002), nevertheless they run counter to the idea that conflict may generate more equal relations between women and men. They surely compromise the potential for achieving change, especially for women in the aftermath of violence. Therefore, it is important to gain more insight into the processes that construct, deconstruct, and reconstruct such gendered images and identities to influence them positively. In the literature studied, masculinity and femininity issues were mentioned, but rarely translated into policy practice. Further studies, particularly policy-relevant ones, are needed to arrive at a deeper understanding of gender's role in conflict.

Closely related to the point above are male gender roles in conflict. Although gender debates focus heavily on women's positions, roles, and identities, little is known about male gender roles in relation to conflict. Male identities, the link between masculinity and violence, the need to derive a nonmilitarized masculinity, and the particular position of adolescents and young men are underexposed subjects in the literature. Although there is anthropological work on these issues, few if any studies have a practical policy focus.

Young Men at Risk

Many commentators note that disillusioned and marginalized young men make up a substantial part of the support base for rebel movements. Although disillusionment and marginalization pay little heed to gender, they are more likely to be manifested as aggressive and violent behavior among young men. As Bessell (2001) noted, the violent and aggressive culture that results often seems impenetrable to outsiders and is viewed with suspicion and fear. Rather than pondering how to draw these young men into a cohesive society, attention tends to focus on control and punishment issues—responses that tend to establish a cycle of exclusion, violent behavior, punishment, greater exclusion and alienation, and further violence. In recent years, however, this approach has started to change.

There has been increasing attention paid to how boys are socialized, to the specific needs and risks that boys and young men face, and to the need to engage boys and men in promoting gender equity (adapted from Barker 2003).[63] Studying and engaging young men from a gender perspective means, among other things, understanding how young men's behavior puts young women at risk. Research from a number of settings has confirmed that adult men's sexual behavior and attitudes are highly related to gender socialization in early childhood and adolescence. Within gender socialization and gender roles, research is increasingly calling attention to the plurality of male gender roles and masculinities, and some have explored and identified alternative versions of male identities, especially how some versions of masculinity are related to certain risk behaviors such as HIV/AIDS and violence.

In some countries in conflict or emerging from conflict, boys and young men also face gender-specific issues, which have not been well researched or understood. Violence accounts for one-quarter of all male deaths in Colombia and a staggering 60 percent of deaths for males aged 15–44 years. Males of all ages are four times more likely than females to die as a result of homicide (Correia 2003). In El Salvador and Guatemala, the phenomenon of street gangs (*maras*), a mostly male phenomenon, has been one result of urban displacement, migration, unemployment, and perceived lack of social status. The lack of alternative economic opportunities for young men (and young women) thus becomes the precursor for additional violence and conflict in gender-specific ways (Barker 2003). Few if any studies have explored how boys' socialization, their lack of employment or other meaningful roles in society, and the lack of social capital in post-conflict settings relate to young men's participation in violence and other forms of anti-social behavior. There are even fewer suggestions on practical approaches or policy recommendations to address this issue.[64]

Is There a Gender Dimension in Reintegrating Child Soldiers?

In recent years, an estimated 300,000 child soldiers were involved in armed conflicts. When the Ugandan National Resistance Army arrived in Kampala in 1986 with children as young as four among their ranks, they caught the world's attention. Conflicts in Cambodia, Liberia,

Mozambique, and other countries drew attention to the use of child soldiers (Verhey 2001; CPR 2002). Boys are often trained in killing, forced to kill, and face other traumatic experiences in witnessing or being victimized by conflict, yet there appears to be relatively little discussion of gender on child soldiers. For example, some literature suggests that boys and young men are more likely than girls not to talk about emotions and personal problems and may have difficulties admitting or seeking help for mental trauma. There are further suggestions that boys are also more likely than girls to externalize trauma and stress in the form of aggression, which implies gender-specific difficulties in post-conflict reintegration. By now, reviews and analyses of DDR programs call for special attention to girls but seldom mention boys' gender-specific needs. Barker (2003) argues that, for the most part, the gender of boys tends to disappear in most analyses of child soldiers and post-conflict reintegration.

Gender and Other Differential Factors

Future studies should pay more attention to the linkage of gender and ethnicity, religion, language, and the like in conflict (El-Bushra et al. 2002). In particular, case studies may help to assess gender's relative importance compared to other identity markers in shaping women's and men's roles and relationships in conflict-affected areas. This would help to avoid generalizations about the chances of women and men in conflict situations fulfilling certain positions. Not all women enter the informal labor market during conflict—not all men have similar opportunities to participate in formal peace processes. It may also help agencies to better define their target groups in conflict situations. For example, employment programs may opt not to target all women in the area, focusing instead on women of a certain ethnic background that gives them the most marginal access to employment.

Macroeconomic Policies and Institution Building in Post-Conflict Settings

Although there are increasing attempts to examine the gender impact of macroeconomic policies and reforms, there has been scarce analytical work on post-conflict macroeconomic policies and engendering institution and capacity building in reconstruction processes. Zuckerman and Greenberg (2004) point out that in an increasing number of post-conflict countries, women are promoting "gender budgets" to monitor how public resources are allocated and spent. They argue that gender budget exercises are likely to result in national spending that promotes gender equality and enhances accountability, transparency, and democracy. They also argue that "to the extent that gender equality institutionalizes respect and tolerance, it can play a positive role in institution-building." Additional research is needed to document these experiences and determine the impacts.

Rebuilding an effective state and creating accountable institutions are key tasks in most post-conflict reconstruction processes. Designing and implementing gender-responsive policies depends on developing appropriate institutional capacity, while a well-functioning state forms the framework where social cohesion needs to be developed. However, Bessell (2001) argues that a post-conflict focus on good governance is not enough to encourage greater social cohesion and gender balance. Instead, reconsidering the governance agenda would entail a shift away from an exclusive emphasis on governance processes and institutions, toward recognition of the importance of social relationships and their connections to political and economic structures. In most post-conflict reconstruction efforts, especially when there are severe socioeconomic constraints, there is a tendency to promote separate units within government ministries and agencies to provide segregated women's services as the only workable strategy. However, this can result in limited, small-scale women's programs or initiatives that are peripheral to mainstream activities and the broader development effort (adapted from Social Development Department 1995). A more systematic gender approach to institution building in conflict settings would seem to offer better prospects for genuine gender mainstreaming in post-conflict reconstruction.[65] Overall, how to engender state and institution building in post-conflict reconstruction is an issue that deserves greater analysis.

Linking Gender, Conflict, and Development Cooperation

There is a risk that the interrelationship between gender, conflict, and development will become a separate research topic in itself. However, it would be more useful if studies capitalized on existing insights in the gender, conflict, and development cooperation fields. Gender studies, particularly those from a feminist perspective, may further highlight how militarized conflict situations reduce the scope for more equal gender relations. Conflict studies could analyze in greater detail how gender roles in conflict differ from gender roles in nonconflict situations.

They could also explain better the potential differences between gender-sensitization efforts in conflict-affected areas and those in stable situations. Insights in the development cooperation field could prevent agencies working in conflict from reinventing the wheel. The development cooperation literature is full of experiences of working to improve women's and men's more equal access to land, to labor markets, to the political arena, to the police, or to legal institutions. Hence, this literature may help agencies to adjust these lessons and best practices to conflict situations. All in all, future studies must combine better the existing insights in these three fields to come to a more informed analysis on the interrelationship of gender, conflict, and development.

Social Capital, Cohesion, and Gender

Social cohesion is the key intervening variable between social capital and violent conflict. The greater the degree to which vertical linking and horizontal social capital integrate, the more likely that a society will be cohesive and have the inclusive mechanisms needed to mediate or manage conflict before it turns violent. When these mediating mechanisms fail and combine with other enabling factors, violent intrastate conflict is likely. As conflict itself further erodes social capital and cohesion, post-conflict reconstruction and the establishment of lasting peace require building or rebuilding social cohesion. Social cohesion and conflict analyses regularly explore various cleavages within society—ethnic, religious, economic, caste, or class-based—but remarkably little research and policy attention have been paid to the gender dimensions of social capital and social cohesion.[66] How do gender roles undermine social cohesion? How can gender roles be harnessed to promote social cohesion? Although social networks can exacerbate a gender divide and marginalize women in relation to the most powerful and dominant groups in society, bridging social capital has powerful potential to heal and unite societies.

This review found little if any systematic analysis of the gender dimensions of social capital and cohesion, which suggests that it is a seriously underdeveloped and underresearched topic. The exceptions are Bessell (2001), who argues that women's groups can play a leading role in bridging social capital, and Zuckerman and Greenberg (2004), who argue that taking care to avoid previous gender-based roles and purposefully promoting gender equality are ways to build new social relationships horizontally rather than vertically through command chains. Although the women's role frequently rates a passing mention in some social capital literature, it tends to be superficial and perfunctory, generally pointing approvingly to the emergence and participation of women's groups in various forms of post-conflict communal action. At the same time, there is an emerging although still tentative body of work, mainly based on individual case studies, on women's participation in reintegration and community-based post-conflict reconstruction efforts. However, these experiences have yet to be systematized and fully incorporated into the analytical frameworks used to analyze social capital and social cohesion.

More Attention to Transformative Approaches

Finally, parallel to practical activities to engage women and men equally in reconstruction activities, there seems to be a strong need for transformative approaches that can fundamentally alter the balance of power in gender relations as post-conflict societies rebuild. Changing this balance is a complex long-term undertaking, a process that many Western societies are still engaged in. More transformative approaches involve a wide range of gender-related issues, from equality in laws or regulations and their implementation, to practical steps to require or encourage gender equality, coupled with information dissemination and sensitization campaigns. Monitoring and evaluation of such activities are important to learn how they affect or contribute to achieving these broader transformations.

Notes

1. In this report, no justice could be done to the many useful contributions by recent feminist conceptualizations of security and violence; see Hudson (1998) and Enloe (2000). They argue for a comprehensive and multilevel approach to the various dimensions of the debate and provide critical insight into the masculine and militaristic underpinnings of much of the international relations, conflict, and peace studies literature. However, this would have opened an epistemological debate beyond this review's scope.

2. There have been several initiatives to monitor and follow up the Platform for Action and Security Council Resolution 1325, and further studies have been undertaken to analyze the interrelationship between gender, conflict, and peace. See UN (2002) and Rehn and Sirleaf (2002).

3. To gender reality in this context means that processes (and institutions) have an impact on gender relations and how they affect men and women differently because of their gender.

4. Gendered analysis implies looking at the roles of both men and women—not just the negative effects on women—and analyzing men's roles and how they interact due to gender.

5. This includes masculine traits such as being aggressive, ambitious, ruthless, and confrontational.

6. Actors or individuals are not prisoners of their history, culture, and so on, but interpret and negotiate social relations. The opposite of actor orientation would imply that there is not much that individuals can do because they cannot escape from the constraints of existing social norms, values, culture, and the like.

7. For an analysis of 'women warriors,' see Goldstein (2001).

8. Barth (2002), quoting Kriger (1992), Turshen and Twagiramariya (1998), and Arthur (1998).

9. Barth (2002), quoting Arthur (1998), Brock-Utne (1987), and Menkhaus and Prendergast (1999).

10. UN (2002), Barth (2002), quoting Zimbabwe Women's Writers (2000).

11. See de Watteville (2002), Barth (2002), Farr (2002), BICC (2002a), and UNDDA (2001, 2003).

12. Arthy (2003) estimates that delivering a broader reintegration program in Sierra Leone, covering the 50,000 ex-combatants plus an estimated additional 50,000 war-affected youth and women, would have required up to $135 million. While the cost appears high, he argues it should be compared to the $3-4 billion spent on UNAMSIL's short-term stabilization efforts.

13. de Watteville (2002). See also Hilhorst (2001) for more specific information on gender-sensitizing Eritrea's second demobilization and reintegration process.

14. The authors acknowledge the importance of political reintegration efforts but it is not discussed because of lack of information in the literature reviewed.

15. Bennett et al. (1995) and Kingma (1997) indicate how ex-soldiers in Mozambique had to be ritually cleansed to be accepted by the community. For more information, see also www.cfr.org/background/liberia_kids.php, or www.africaaction.org/docs99/viol9907.htm.

16. See Colletta et al. (1996), UNDDA (2001), and Farr (2002).

17. Goldstein (2001) questions the high numbers of civilian casualties in war and questions the assumption that more women are victims than men. However, his data are derived from both interstate and intrastate conflicts.

18. Corrin (2004) argues that viewing trafficking primarily as a migration or national security issue and not as a human rights violation has consequences for criminalizing trafficking victims. Feminist human rights activists support decriminalization with a human rights approach.

19. See Carballo et al. (2000) for a more detailed analysis of the link between HIV/AIDS prevention and the demobilization and reintegration processes.

20. See, among others, the Web site http://www.usofficepristina.usia.co.at/kwi/kwi10.htm.

21. See OSCE (2001), ICRC (2001), UNFPA (2002), and http://www.iom.ipko.org/Counter_trafficking/counter_trafficking.htm#IOM.

22. Indigenous healing and rituals contrast with Western modes addressing trauma, which tend to psychotherapeutic recounting and remembering experiences. Indigenous approaches tend to emphasize a rupture with the past and cleansing. See McKay and Mazurana (2004).

23. WHO (2000) and Reproductive Health Outlook at www.rho.org/html/refugee_progexamples.htm#tanzania.

24. WHO/UNHCR (2002), quoting "Workshop Report: The Challenge of Rebuilding War-torn Societies and the Social Consequences of the Peace Process in Cambodia," Geneva, September 1993.

25. See, among others, United Nations Children's Fund (UNICEF)/UNOHCHR/OSCE-ODIHR (2002), IOM (2001, 2002).

26. Personal communication with Mrs. Zimmerman, former ODIHR gender adviser.

27. For more detailed recommendations regarding the combat of trafficking, see IOM (2002).

28. Like female rape, sexual violence against men should be conceptualized as "an exercise in power, domination, and humiliation, rather than a pure sexual act" (Nordang 2002, quoting El-Bushra and Piza-Lopez 1993). Indeed men are often raped in times of conflict to "feminize" them—to "reduce" them to the status of women (Nordang 2002).

29. van Tienhoven (1992). For further reading on sexual violence against men, see also van Tienhoven (1993).

30. Porter (2003) points out that there were no Bosnian women in the negotiating teams in Dayton in 1995; there was only one Kosova woman at the Rambouillet negotiations in 1999; in Tajikistan there was only one woman on a 26-person National Reconciliation Commission; Concilie Nibigiri was the only woman present at the Arusha peace talks on Burundi—the women's collective, which included 30 organizations, negotiated the presence of six women with observer status at the next round. The Liberian Women's Initiative attended regional peace talks but were not official participants (although they were influential monitors); the Consultative Council of Timorese Resistance had two women representatives out of 15; and in December 2001, there were three Afghani women out of 36 delegates to the Bonn negotiations. In Colombia, there were only four women among approximately 40 participants in the official process of negotiations under the Pastrana Administration. Under pressure from the women leaders involved in the talks, however, the parties agreed to hold a women's public forum, which culminated in a day-long event where 600 women participated, which, in turn, put pressure on the parties to acknowledge that their own forces had committed GBV (Rojas 2004).

31. Caprioli (2003) argues that fertility rates and women in the legislature are the two best measures to capture the complex matrix of gender discrimination and inequality that includes political, economic, and social discrimination. Because of data limitations, fertility rates are included in the final models as a measure of gender inequality.

32. International Peace Research Institute of Oslo, Norway, and the University of Uppsala, Sweden.

33. See www.stabilitypact.org.

34. UNIFEM East and Southeast Asia, www.unifem.org/www/global_ spanner/e_se_asia.html.

35. It would be interesting to consider and further analyze the World Bank's role in supporting these kinds of CSOs.

36. In Somalia (Puntland), women have tried to develop local initiatives to draw youth away from militias despite threats from traditional power structures (as reported to a World Bank team conducting a conflict assessment in Puntland).

37. S. Anderson (1999) quotes Women in Black (1994): "Since the beginning of the war most members of pacifist organizations have been women. Women's participation in such organizations is taken for granted in the sense that activities such as caring for others, healing the wounded, giving shelter and consolation are considered their 'natural' role. Having realized that these feminine traits are misused in a militarist society such as ours and that even the democratic opposition and the peace movement repeat patriarchal models, we decide to make our resistance to war public—not as a part of our 'natural' role but as a conscious political choice."

38. See Sörensen (1998), International Alert (2000), Naraghi Anderlini (2000), Femmes Afrique Solidarité (2000), Kumar (2001), NUPI (2001), UN (2002), Rehn and Sirleaf (2002), Strickland and Duvvury (2003), and UNDP (2003).

39. Weiss Fagen and Yudelman (2001). For more background information, particularly on the co-ownership of land issue, see also Worby (2001).

40. In Georgia, most female civil society leaders were reluctant to enter formal politics, stating that political parties were not sensitive to their needs and that their organizations could be more effective if they remained politically independent (Morton et al. 2001).

41. For an overview of other relevant laws, see UN (2002) and UNDP (2003).

42. In fact, UNIFEM was established to promote CEDAW.

43. For example, Human Rights Watch (2002) clearly shows the struggle of the DRC authorities to respond to GBV.

44. OSCE (2001), IOM (2001, 2002), and UNICEF/UNOHCHR/OSCE-ODIHR (2002).

45. Goldstein (2001), for instance, provides ample evidence of the exploitation, as he calls it, of women's work during conflict, trying to test the hypothesis that women cannot generally become warriors because their work must keep the war machine running. However, his conclusion is that this is only modestly the case.

46. Colletta et al. (1996) show how returning ex-soldiers in Ethiopia, Namibia, and Uganda faced such challenges in obtaining access to land and in attempting to reintegrate economically in rural areas. However, they do not indicate whether female and male ex-soldiers faced different challenges.

47. Walsh (1997), Sörensen (1998), quoting Barron (1996), Cheater and Gaidzanwa (1996), ILO (1995), Sogge (1992), and War Report (1995). See also Vincent (2001), ILO (1997, 1998, 2001), Kumar (2001), Farr (2002), and de Watteville (2002).

48. Byrne (1996), Baden (1997), Kumar (2000), Machel (2000), OSCE (2001), ICRC (2001), and Barth (2002).

49. ILO (1998), quoting Baden (1997).

50. Walsh (1997, 2001) and Date-Bah and Walsh (2001).

51. Byrne (1996), ICRC (2001), Woroniuk (2001), and UN (2002).

52. See, for instance, WHO/UNFPA/UNHCR (1999), WHO (2000), ICRC (2001), and WHO/UNHCR (2002).

53. Ongoing World Bank research (Barron et al. 2003) is attempting to test whether communities in Indonesia that benefited from a CDD approach are, indeed, better able to channel conflict constructively. A particular feature of this research is that it is attempting comparisons between villages where a CDD approach operated for three years and statistically comparable villages where CDD approaches were not present.

54. Communication with Ms. Nani Zulminarni (Center for the Development of Women's Resources, Indonesia), and UNDESA (2001)—the latter has had comprehensive discussions of the special problems faced by widows, especially in post-conflict settings.

55. Communication with Ms. Nani Zulminarni (Center for the Development of Women's Resources, Indonesia).

56. Communication with Ms. Enurlaela Hasanah (World Bank, Jakarta Office).

57. The World Bank's Social Development Department developed social analysis guidelines (Social Development Department 2003). Bank social scientists use five entry points or dimensions of inquiry to undertake a social analysis, one of which is social diversity and gender.

58. Communication with Ms. Nani Zulminarni (Center for the Development of Women's Resources, Indonesia).

59. Personal communication with Scott Guggenheim (World Bank, Jakarta Office).

60. For instance Turner (1999), using a case study on Burundian refugees in Tanzania, interestingly shows how promoting gender equality does not automatically imply that anything like equality between the sexes will be achieved.

61. Personal communication with Mrs. Dubravka Zarkov, Senior Lecturer on Gender, Conflict, and Development at the Institute of Social Studies in The Hague, The Netherlands.

62. Marcelo Fabre argues there is a need for internationally agreed policy guidance and accepted principles to define the female "combatant" and therefore the beneficiary target of DDR operations. He draws a parallel with the situation of child soldiers where, before the Pretoria protocols, strict eligibility criteria left child combatants out of DDR benefits (personal communication).

63. The 1994 International Conference on Population and Development and the 1995 Fourth World Conference on Women in Beijing provided a foundation for incorporating men—including young men—in efforts to improve women's status, including in the sexual and reproductive health areas.

64. Related to the point above, although not always apparent in a conflict setting is the even less researched topic of female youth. Successfully reaching young females is a persistent and particularly thorny challenge in youth programming. As Sommers (2003) points out, it is more common to find male youth associated with the term "youth" than female youth, who may simply be considered "young women." A related problem arises when female youth are married—are they still youth or are they mainly young mothers? The tendency for urban male youth to live much more public and violent lives than urban female youth makes reaching them through effective programs and interventions much more challenging.

65. In El Salvador, the National Center for Agricultural and Forestry Technology conducted a program with World Bank support to adopt a more systematic gender approach. It eliminated its women's program in 1994 and attempted to incorporate gender systematically into planning, monitoring, training, extension, and research, and modified its organizational structure to ensure that gender issues were addressed effectively. Although preliminary reports suggested that the Center was able to increase women's participation in its extension programs, there is no comprehensive evaluation of this approach (Social Development Department 1995).

66. An important neglected dimension is the incorporation of gender in conflict assessments and early warning indicators. Most frameworks that international agencies use to better understand conflict risks rarely include a mention of gender aspects.

Bibliography

de Abreu, A. A. 1998. Mozambican Women Experiencing Violence. In *What Women do in Wartime: Gender and Conflict in Africa*, eds. M. Turshen, and C. Twagiramariya, 73–84. London: Zed Books.

Amnesty International. 2003. *Afghanistan: Police Reconstruction Essential for the Protection of Human Rights*. London: Amnesty International.

Anderson, M. B. 1999. *Do No Harm: How Aid Can Support Peace or War*. Boulder, Colo., and London: Lynne Rienner.

Anderson, S. 1999. Women's Many Roles in Reconciliation. In *People Building Peace: 35 Inspiring Stories from Around the World*: 230–236. Utrecht: European Centre for Conflict Prevention.

Arthur, M. J. 1998. Mozambique: Women in the Armed Struggle. In *Southern Africa in Transition: A Gendered Perspective*, ed. P. McFadden, 67–82. Harare: Sapes.

Arthy, S. 2003. Ex Combatant Reintegration: Key Issues for Policy Makers and Practitioners, Based on Lessons from Sierra Leone. Working paper, DfID, London.

Astgeirsdottir, K. 2002. Women and Girls in Kosovo: The Effect of Armed Conflict on the Lives of Women. In UNFPA, *The Impact of Conflict on Women and Girls: A UNFPA Strategy for Gender Mainstreaming in Areas of Conflict and Reconstruction*: 77–102. Bratislava: UNFPA, 2002.

Baden, S. 1997. Post-Conflict Mozambique: Women's Special Situation, Population Issues and Gender Perspectives. Report 44. Brighton: IDS/BRIDGE.

Baker, J. M., and H. Haug. 2002. Independent Evaluation of the Kosovo Women's Initiative: Executive Summary. Geneva: UNHCR.

Barker, G. 2002. Growing Up Poor and Male in the Americas: Reflections from Research and Practice with Young Men in Low Income Communities in Rio de Janeiro, Brazil. Working paper.

———. 2003. Young Men At-Risk: A Concept Paper and Plan of Action. Working paper, PROMUNDO, Rio de Janeiro.

Barnes, C. 2002. Democratizing Peacemaking Processes: Strategies and Dilemmas for Public Participation. Conciliation Resources/Accord. www.cr.org/accord/peace/accord13/intro.shtml.

Barron, M. 1996. When the Soldiers Come Home: A Gender Analysis of the Reintegration of Demobilized Soldiers, Mozambique 1994–1996. Master's Thesis, University of East Anglia.

Barron, P., R. Diprose, D. Madden, C. Smith, and M. Woolcock. 2003. Do Participatory Development Projects Help Villagers Manage Local Conflicts? Social Development Papers: Conflict Prevention & Reconstruction, CPR Working Paper No. 9, World Bank, Washington, DC.

Barth, E. F. 2002. *Peace as Disappointment: The Reintegration of Female Soldiers in Post-Conflict Societies. A Comparative Study from Africa.* Oslo: PRIO.

Beijing Declaration and Platform for Action. 1995. Adopted by the Fourth World Conference on Women: Action for Equality, Development and Peace. Working paper.

Bennett, O., J. Bexley, and K. Warnock. 1995. *Arms to Fight, Arms to Protect: Women Speak Out about Conflict.* London: PANOS.

Bessell, S. 2001. Social Capital and Conflict Management: Rethinking the Issues Using a Gender-Sensitive Lens. In *Social Cohesion and Conflict Prevention in Asia,* eds. N. Colletta, T. Ghee Lim, and A. Kelles-Viitanen. Washington, DC: World Bank.

BICC (Bonn International Center for Conversion). 2002. Veteran Combatants Do Not Fade Away: A Comparative Study on Two Demobilization and Reintegration Exercises in Eritrea. Paper 23. Bonn: BICC.

———. 2002a. Gender Perspectives on Small Arms and Light Weapons: Regional and International Concerns. Brief 24. Bonn: BICC.

Bop, C. 2001. Women in Conflicts: Their Gains and Their Losses. In *The Aftermath: Women in Post-Conflict Transformation,* eds. S. Meintjes, A. Pillay, and M. Turshen, 19–33. New York: Zed Books.

Bouta, T., and G. Frerks. 2001. The Role of SNV (Dutch Development Agency) in Developing Countries in Internal Armed Conflict. Report written for The Netherlands Technical Assistance Cooperation Organization SNV, Clingendael, The Hague.

———, eds. 2002. Women's Roles in Conflict Prevention, Conflict Resolution and Post-Conflict Reconstruction: Literature Review and Institutional Analysis. Report written for the Ministry of Social Affairs and Employment, Clingendael, The Hague.

———. 2003. Engendering Peace and Conflict. In *Cannons and Canons: Clingendael Views of Global and Regional Politics,* eds. A. van Staden, J. Rood, and H. Labohm, 290–307. Assen: Royal Van Gorcum.

Brett, R., and I. Specht. 2004. Forthcoming. *Young Soldiers, Why they Choose to Fight.* Boulder, Colo., and London: Lynne Rienner.

Brittain, V. 2002. Women and War and Crisis Zones: One Key to Africa's Wars of Underdevelopment. Working Paper 21, London School of Economics/Development Research Center, London.

Brock-Utne, B. 1987. *Educating for Peace: A Feminist Perspective*. New York: Pergamon.

Bruchhaus, E. M., and A. Mehreteab. 2000. 'Leaving the 'Warm House': The Impact of Demobilization in Eritrea. In *Demobilization in Sub-Sahara Africa: The Development and Security Impacts*, ed. K. Kingma, 95–131. London: Macmillan Press.

Byrne, B. 1996. Gender, Conflict and Development. Volumes I and II. Report prepared for The Netherlands Ministry of Foreign Affairs, Institute of Development Studies, Brighton.

Caprioli, M. 2000. Gendered Conflict. *Journal of Peace Research* 37(1): 51–68.

———. 2003. Gender Equality and Civil Wars. Social Development Papers: Conflict Prevention & Reconstruction, CPR Working Paper No. 8, World Bank, September, Washington, DC.

Carballo, M., C. Mansfield, and M. Prokop. 2000. *Demobilization and its Implications for HIV/AIDS*. Geneva: International Center for Health and Migration (ICMH).

Cheater, A.P., and R.B. Gaidzanwa. 1996. Citizenship in Neo-Patrilineal States: Gender and Mobility in Southern Africa. *Journal of Southern African Studies* 22(2): 189–200.

Cliffe, S., S. Guggenheim, and M. Kostner. 2003. Community-Driven Reconstruction as an Instrument in War-to-Peace Transitions. CPR Working Papers, Paper No. 7, August, World Bank, Washington, DC.

Cock, J. 2001. *Closing the Circle: Toward a Gendered Understanding of War and Peace*. http://www.uct.ac.za/org/agi/newslet/vol8/lead.htm.

Cockburn, C. 1998. *The Space between Us: Negotiating Gender and National Identities in Conflict*. London and New York: Zed Books.

Cockburn, C., and D. Zarkov, eds. 2002. *The Postwar Moment: Militaries, Masculinities and International Peacekeeping*. London: Lawrence & Wishart.

Colletta, N., and M. Cullen. 2000. *Violent Conflict and the Transformation of Social Capital: Lessons from Cambodia, Rwanda, Guatemala, and Somalia*. Washington, DC: World Bank.

Colletta, N., M. Kostner, and I. Wiederhofer. 1996. Case Studies in War-to-Peace Transition: The Demobilization and Reintegration of Ex-Combatants in Ethiopia, Namibia and Uganda. World Bank Discussion Paper 331. Africa Technical Department Series, World Bank, Washington, DC.

———. 1996a. *The Transition from War to Peace in Sub-Saharan Africa*. Washington, DC: World Bank.

Conaway, C. P., and S. Martínez. 2004. *Adding Value: Women's Contributions to Reintegration and Reconstruction in El Salvador*. With contributions from S. Gammage and E. Piza-Lopez. Women Waging Peace Policy Commission: Hunt Alternatives Fund.

Correia, M. 2003. Gender. In *Colombia: The Economic Foundation of Peace*, eds. M. Guigale, O. Lafourcade, and C. Luff. Washington, DC: World Bank.

Corrin, C. 2004. International and Local Interventions to Reduce Gender-Based Violence against Women in Post-Conflict Situations. Paper presented at the UNU-WIDER Conference on Making Peace Work, Helsinki, June 2004.

CPR (Conflict Prevention and Reconstruction). 2000. Child Soldiers: Prevention, Demobilization and Reintegration. Dissemination Notes, No. 3, May, World Bank, Washington, DC.

———. 2002. Conflict and Labor Markets in Manufacturing: The Case of Eritrea. Dissemination Notes, No. 7, December, World Bank Washington, DC.

———. 2004. Social Change in Conflict-Affected Areas of Nepal. Social Development Notes: Conflict Prevention & Reconstruction, No. 15, January, World Bank, Washington, DC.

———. 2004a. Colombia: The Role of Land in Involuntary Displacement. Social Development Notes: Conflict Prevention & Reconstruction, No. 17, March, World Bank, Washington, DC.

———. 2004b. Rwanda: The Impact of Conflict on Growth and Poverty. Social Development Notes: Conflict Prevention & Reconstruction, No. 18, June, World Bank, Washington, DC.

———. 2004c. *The Role of the World Bank in Conflict and Development: An Evolving Agenda*. Social Development Department. Washington, DC: World Bank, Washington, DC.

Dahlerup, D. 2001. Women in Political Decisionmaking: From Critical Mass to Critical Acts in Scandinavia. In *Gender, Peace and Conflict*, eds. I. Skjelsbaek, and D. Smith, 104–121. London: Sage.

Date-Bah, and E. and M. Walsh. 2001. Gender and Conflict: Some Key Issues and Findings from Recent ILO Research. In ILO, *Gender and Armed Conflicts*, Working Paper 2: 1–22. Geneva: ILO.

Education Team (World Bank). 2003. Education in Post-Conflict Reconstruction. Human Development Network, Working Paper, October, World Bank, Washington, DC.

El-Bushra. 2003. Women Building Peace: Sharing Know-How. Report written in the framework of International Alert's Gender and Peace Building Program, International Alert, London.

El-Bushra, J., and E. Piza-Lopez. 1993. Development in Conflict: The Gender Dimension. Report of a Workshop in Thailand, February 1993, Oxfam Discussion Paper 3, Oxfam, Oxford.

El-Bushra, J., A. El-Karib, and A. Hadjipateras. 2002. *Gender-Sensitive Program Design and Planning in Conflict-Affected Situations*. London: ACORD.

Enloe, C. 1998. All the Men are in the Militias, All the Women are Victims. In *The Women and War Reader*, eds. L. A. Lorentzen, and J. Turpin. New York and London: New York University Press.

———. 2000. *Maneuver: The International Politics of Militarizing Women's Lives*. Berkeley CA: University of Los Angeles Press.

FAO (Food and Agriculture Organization). 2002. Gender and Access to Land. FAO Land Tenure Studies 4. Rome: FAO.

Farr, V. 2002. Gendering Demilitarization as a Peace Building Tool. Paper 20, BICC, Bonn.

Femmes Afrique Solidarité. 2000. *Engendering the Peace Process in West Africa: The Mano River Women's Peace Network*. Geneva: Cavin.

Forced Migration (Reproductive Health for Refugee Consortium). 1997. *Refugees and Reproductive Health Care: The Next Step*. New York: Reproductive Health for Refugee Consortium, in http://www.forcedmigration. org/psychosocial.

Frerks, G. E. 2000. Recreating Coherence through the Coherence of Conflict and Disaster: The Role of Local Coping Capacities. Paper presented at the Workshop on New Approaches for the Development of Rural Communities, X Congress for Rural Sociology, Rio de Janeiro.

Fukuyama, F. 1998. Women and the Evolution of World Politics. *Foreign Affairs* 77(5): 24–40.

Galloy, M. R. 2000. Femmes, conflits et paix au congo. Paper prepared for the International Conference on the Transformation of Conflicts in Africa and the Perspectives of African Women, Afard/International Alert, Dakar.

Goldblatt, B., and S. Meintjes. 1998. South African Women Demand the Truth. In *What Women Do in Wartime: Gender and Conflict in Africa*, eds. M. Turshen, and C. Twagiramariya, 27–61. London: Zed Books.

Goldstein, J. S. 2001. *War and Gender: How Gender Shapes the War System and Vice Versa*. Cambridge: Cambridge University Press.

GTZ (Deutsche Gesellschaft für Technische Zusammenarbeit GmbH). 2001. *Toward Gender Mainstreaming in Crisis Prevention and Conflict Management: Guidelines for German Technical Cooperation*. Eschborn: GTZ.

Hale, S. 2001. Liberated, but Not Free: Women in Post-War Eritrea. In *The Aftermath: Women in Post-Conflict Transformation*, eds. S. Meintjes, A. Pillay, and M. Turshen, 122–141. New York: Zed Books.

Hamadeh-Banerjee, L. 2000. Women's Agency in Governance. In UNDP, *Women's Political Participation and Good Governance: Twenty-First Century Challenges:* 7–15. New York: UNDP.

Hamadeh-Banerjee, L., and P. Oquist. 2000. Overview: Women's Political Participation and Good Governance: Twenty-First Century Challenges. In UNDP, *Women's Political Participation and Good Governance: Twenty-First Century Challenges:* 1–6. New York: UNDP.

Hilhorst, D. 2001. Proposal and Recommendations for the Gender Component of the Demobilization and Reintegration Process (DRP). Working paper, based on a visit to Eritrea in January 2001, Wageningen University, Wageningen.

Hilhorst, D., and G. Frerks. 1999. Local Capacities for Peace: Concepts, Possibilities and Constraints. Paper presented at a seminar on Local Capacities for Peace, organized by Pax Christi, Interchurch Peace Council (IKV) and Disaster Studies Wageningen, Utrecht.

Holtzman, S. B., and T. Nezam. 2004. *Living in Limbo: Conflict-Induced Displacement in Europe and Central Asia.* Washington, DC: World Bank.

Hudson, H. 1998. A Feminist Reading of Security in Africa. *Caring Security in Africa.* ISS Monograph 20. www.iss.co.za?Pubs?Monographs/No20/Hudson.html.

Human Rights Watch. 1996. *Shattered Lives: Sexual Violence during the Rwandan Genocide and Its Aftermath.* New York: Human Rights Watch.

———. 2002. *The War within the War: Sexual Violence against Women and Girls in Eastern Congo.* New York: Human Rights Watch.

Ibañez, A. C. 2001. El Salvador: War and Untold Stories. Women Guerrillas. In *Victims, Perpetrators or Actors? Gender, Armed Conflict and Political Violence,* eds. C. O. N. Moser, and F. Clark, 117–140. London and New York: Zed Books.

ICG (International Crisis Group). 2003. Afghanistan: Women and Reconstruction. ICG Asia Report 48, ICG, Kabul and Brussels.

ICRC (International Committee of the Red Cross). 2001. Women Facing War. ICRC Study on the Impact of Armed Conflict on Women, ICRC, Geneva.

———. 2003. Women and War. Special Report, ICRC, Geneva.

ILO. 1995. Reintegrating Demobilized Combatants: Experiences from Four African Countries. Paper prepared for an Expert Meeting on the Design of Guidelines for Training and Employment of Ex-Combatants, Africa Region, Harare, ILO, Geneva.

———. 1997. *Manual on Training and Employment Options for Ex-Combatants.* Geneva: ILO.

———. 1998. *Gender Guidelines for Employment and Skills Training in Conflict-Affected Countries.* Geneva: ILO.

———. 2001. Gender and Armed Conflicts. Working Paper 2, ILO, Geneva.

———. 2001a. Afghan Women: Women's Role in Afghanistan's Reconstruction and Development. Working Paper 4, ILO, Geneva.

Institute for Security Studies (ISS). 2002. *Violence Against Women: A National Survey.* Pretoria: ISS.

International Alert. 2000. Women, Conflict and Peace Building: Global Perspectives. Paper presented at an international conference in London, May 1999, International Alert, London.

————. 2002. *Gender Mainstreaming in Peace Support Operations: Moving Beyond Rhetoric to Practice.* London: International Alert.

International IDEA. 1997. *Women in Politics: Beyond Numbers.* Stockholm: International IDEA.

————. 1998. *Democracy and Deep-Rooted Conflict: Options for Negotiators.* Stockholm: International IDEA.

————. 2002. *Women in Parliament: Beyond Numbers. Updates of Selected Sections and Chapters of the First Edition.* Stockholm: International IDEA.

Inter-Parliamentary Union. 2004. *Women in National Parliaments: World Classification.* Situation as of February 29, 2004. http://www.ipu.org/wmn-e/classif.htm.

IOM (International Office for Migration). 2001. *Victims of Trafficking in the Balkans: A Study of Trafficking in Women and Children for Sexual Exploitation to, through and from the Balkan Region.* Geneva and Vienna: IOM.

————. 2002. *Brussels Declaration on Preventing and Combating Trafficking in Human Beings.* Brussels: IOM.

Jiggins, J. 1986. Gender-Related Impacts and the Work of the International Agricultural Research Centers. CGIAR Study Paper 17, World Bank, Washington, DC.

Julia, M. 1995. Revisiting a Repopulated Village: A Step Backwards in the Changing Status of Women. *International Social Work* 38 (229): 242.

Karame, K. 1999. Women and War: A Highly Complex Interrelation. In NUPI, *Women and Armed Conflicts: A Study for the Norwegian Ministry:* 4–31. Oslo: NUPI.

Kievelitz, U., T. Schaef, M. Leonhardt, H. Hahn, and S. Vorwerk. 2004. Practical Guide to Multilateral Needs Assessments in Post-Conflict Situations. Social Development Papers: Conflict Prevention & Reconstruction, CPR Working Paper 15, prepared by GTZ for the World Bank and UNDG/UNDP, World Bank, Washington, DC.

Kingma, K. 1996. *The Role of Demobilization in the Peace and Development Process in Sub-Saharan Africa: Conditions for Success.* http://www.iss.co.za/Pubs/ASR/5No6/Kingma.html.

————. 1997. Post-War Demobilization and the Reintegration of Ex-Combatants in Civilian Life. In *After the War Is Over, What Comes Next?* A compilation by Nicole Ball of 14 papers presented at an October 1997 conference promoting democracy, human rights and reintegration in post-conflict societies, USAID, Washington, DC.

————. 2000. Assessing Demobilization: Conceptual Issues. In *Demobilization in Sub-Saharan Africa: The Development and Security Impacts,* ed. K. Kingma, 23–44. London: Macmillan.

Kriger, N. J. 1992. *Zimbabwe's Guerrilla War: Peasant Voices.* Cambridge: Cambridge University Press.

Kritz, N. J. 1997. War Crimes and Truth Commissions: Some Thoughts on Accountability Mechanisms for Mass Violations of Human Rights. In *After the War Is Over, What Comes Next?* A compilation by Nicole Ball of 14 papers presented at an October 1997 conference on promoting democracy, human rights and reintegration in post-conflict societies, USAID, Washington, DC.

Kumar, K. 2000. *Women and Women's Organizations in Post-Conflict Societies: The Role of International Assistance.* Washington, DC: USAID.

———, ed. 2001. *Women and Civil War: Impact, Organizations and Action.* Boulder, Colo., and London: Lynne Rienner.

Kumar, K., and H. Baldwin. 2001. Women's Organizations in Post-conflict Cambodia. In *Women and Civil War: Impact, Organizations and Action,* edited by K. Kumar, 129–138. Boulder, Colo., and London: Lynne Rienner.

Kvinna till Kvinna. 2000. *Engendering the Peace Process: A Gender Approach to Dayton—and Beyond.* Stockholm: Kvinna till Kvinna.

———. 2001. *Getting it Right? A Gender Approach to UNMIK Administration in Kosovo.* Stockholm: Kvinna till Kvinna.

———. 2002. *War Is Not Over with the Last Bullet: Overcoming Obstacles in the Healing Process of Women in Bosnia-Herzegovina.* Stockholm: Kvinna till Kvinna.

Limura, T., and M. Kawamo. Women's Participation in KDP. Working paper, World Bank, Jakarta.

Lindsey, C. 2002. Women and War. Geneva: ICRC.

Long, N. 1997. Agency and Constraint, Perceptions and Practice. A Theoretical Position. In *Images and Realities of Rural Life: Wageningen Perspectives on Rural Transformation,* eds. H. de Haan and N. Long, 1–20. Assen: Van Gorcum.

Long, N., and J. D. van der Ploeg. 1989. Demythologizing Planned Intervention: An Actor Perspective. *Sociologia Ruralis* 29(3/4): 226–249.

Loufti, M. F., ed. 2001. *Women, Gender and Work.* Geneva: ILO.

Machel, G. 2000. *International Conference on War-Affected Children: The Impact of Armed Conflict on Children. A Critical Review of Progress Made and Obstacles Encountered in Increasing Protection of War-Affected Children.* Winnipeg, Canada: UNIFEM and UNICEF.

Manchanda, R., ed. 2001. *Women, War and Peace in South Asia: Beyond Victimhood to Agency.* New Delhi: Sage Productions.

Manoharan, N. 2003. *Tigresses of Lanka: From Girls to Guerillas.* Institute of Peace and Conflict Studies, Article No. 1001. http//www.icps.org.

Marques, J., and I. Bannon. 2003. Central America: Education Reform in a Post-Conflict Setting, Opportunities and Challenges. Conflict Prevention and Reconstruction Unit Working Papers, No. 4, World Bank, Washington, DC.

Mazurana, D., and K. Carlson. 2004. *From Combat to Community: Women and Girls of Sierra Leone.* With contributions by S. Naraghi Anderlini. Women Waging Peace Policy Commission: Hunt Alternatives Fund.

McGrew, L., K. Frierson, and S. Chan. 2004. *Good Governance from the Ground Up: Women's Roles in Post-Conflict Cambodia.* Women Waging Peace Commission: Hunt Alternatives Fund.

McKay, S., and D. Mazurana. 2004. *Where Are the Girls? Girls in Fighting Forces in Northern Uganda, Sierra Leone and Mozambique: Their Lives during and after War.* Canada: Rights & Democracy.

Meenakshi, S. 2003. Gender and Conflict in Bank-Funded Operations and Strategies. Working paper, prepared for the East Asia Environment and Social Development Department of the World Bank.

Meertens, D. 2001. The Nostalgic Future: Terror, Displacement and Gender in Colombia. In *Victims, Perpetrators or Actors? Gender, Armed Conflict and Political Violence,* eds. C. O. N. Moser and F. Clark, 133–147. London and New York: Zed Books.

Meintjes, S. 1998. Gender, Nationalism and Transformation: Difference and Commonality in South Africa's Past and Present. In *Women, Ethnicity and Nationalism: The Politics of Transition,* eds. R. Wilford and R. L. Miller, 62–86. London: Routledge.

Meintjes, S., A. Pillay, and M. Turshen, eds. 2001. *The Aftermath: Women in Post-Conflict Transformation.* New York: Zed Books.

———. 2001a. There Is No Aftermath for Women. In *The Aftermath: Women in Post-Conflict Transformation,* eds. S. Meintjes, A. Pillay, and M. Turshen, 3–17. New York: Zed Books.

Menkhaus, K. and J. Prendergast. 1999. Conflict and Crisis in the Greater Horn of Africa. *Current History* 98(638): 213–217.

Morton, A. L., S. A. Nan, T. Buck, and F. Zurikashvili. 2001. Georgia in Transition: Women's Organizations and Empowerment. In *Women and Civil War: Impact, Organizations and Action,* ed. K. Kumar, 149–165. Boulder, Colo., and London: Lynne Rienner.

Moser, C. O. N., and C. McIlwaine. 2000. *Urban Poor Perceptions of Violence and Exclusion in Colombia.* Washington, DC: World Bank.

———. 2001. Gender and Social Capital in Contexts of Political Violence: Community Perceptions from Colombia and Guatemala. In *Victims, Perpetrators or Actors? Gender, Armed Conflict and Political Violence,* eds. C. O. N. Moser, and F. Clark. London and New York: Zed Books.

Mukiibi, B. 2000. Alliances for Gender and Politics: The Uganda Caucus. In UNDP, *Women's Political Participation and Good Governance: Twenty-First Century Challenges:* 59–63. New York: UNDP.

Naraghi Anderlini, S. B. 2000. *Women at the Peace Table: Making a Difference.* New York: UNIFEM.

Nauphal, N. 1997. *Post-War Lebanon: Women and Other War-Affected Groups.* Geneva: ILO.

Newbury, V., and H. Baldwin. 2001. Confronting the Aftermath of Conflict: Women's Organizations in Post-Genocide Rwanda. In *Women and Civil War: Impact, Organizations and Action,* ed. K. Kumar, 97–129. Boulder, Colo., and London: Lynne Rienner.

Nordang, H. 2002. Gender and Post-Conflict Reconstruction: The Political Transition from War to Peace in Bosnia and Herzegovina and Implications for Post-Conflict Citizenship. Dissertation in partial fulfillment for a Master of Philosophy Degree in Development Studies, Institute of Development Studies, University of Sussex.

Nordstrom, C. 1991. Women and War: Observations from the Field. *Minerva: Quarterly Report on Women and the Military 9.*

NUPI (Norwegian Institute of International Affairs). 2001. Gendering Human Security: From Marginalization to the Integration of Women in Peace Building. Recommendations for Policy and Practice from the NUPI-FAFO Forum on Gender Relations in Post-Conflict Transitions, NUPI-Report 261, NUPI and FAFO, Oslo.

Nyirankundabera, J. 2002. Annex 6: Complementary Study on Rwanda. In *Gender-Sensitive Program Design and Planning in Conflict-Affected Situations,* eds. J. El-Bushra, A. El-Karib, and A. Hadjipateras. London: ACORD.

OECD/DAC (Organisation for Economic Co-operation and Development/ Development Assistance Committee). 1998. *DAC Guidelines for Gender Equality and Women's Empowerment in Development Cooperation.* Paris: OECD/DAC.

Oklahoma, P. 1999. *Disarmament, Demobilization and Reintegration of Ex-Combatants in a Peacekeeping Environment: Principles and Guidelines.* New York: Department for Peacekeeping Operations/Lessons Learned Unit.

OSCE (Organization for Security and Economic Cooperation in Europe). 2001. Gender Aspects in Post-Conflict Situations: A Guide for OSCE Staff. By the Gender Adviser's Office of the Secretary-General, OSCE, Vienna.

Ostergaard, L. 2003. East Timor Community Empowerment and Local Governance Project. Local Governance and Institutional Development: Independent Review. Working paper, Nordic Consulting Group, Taastrup, Denmark.

Pankhurst, D. 2000. Women, Gender and Peace Building, Working Paper 5. Centre for Conflict Resolution, Department of Peace Studies, University of Bradford, Bradford.

Porter, E. 2003. Women, Political Decision-Making, and Peace-Building. *Global Change, Peace & Security,* 15:3 (October).

Powley, E. 2003. *Strengthening Governance: The Role of Women in Rwanda's Transition.* Women Waging Peace Commission: Hunt Alternatives Fund.

Rehn, E., and E. J. Sirleaf. 2002. *Women, War and Peace: The Independent Expert's Assessment on the Impact of Armed Conflict on Women and Women's Role in Peace-Building.* New York: UNIFEM.

Richards, P., K. Bah, and J. Vincent. 2004. Social Capital and Survival: Prospects for Community-Driven Development in Post-War Sierra Leone. Social Development Papers: Community Driven Development and Conflict Prevention & Reconstruction, No. 12, World Bank, Washington, DC.

Rojas, C. 2004. *In the Midst of War: Women's Contributions to Peace in Colombia.* With S. Naraghi Anderlini and C. P. Conaway. Women Waging Peace Policy Commission: Hunt Alternatives Fund.

Royal Tropical Institute (KIT). 1995. Advancing Women's Status: Gender, Society and Development. Women and Men Together? Critical Reviews and Annotated Bibliography Series. Amsterdam: Royal Tropical Institute, Amsterdam.

Saferworld/International Alert. 2004. *Strengthening Global Security through Addressing the Root Causes of Conflict: Priorities for the Irish and Dutch Presidencies in 2004.* London: International Alert and Saferworld.

Save the Children. 2003. *State of the World's Mothers 2003: Protecting Women and Children in War and Conflict.* London: Save the Children.

Schmeidl, S., and E. Piza-Lopez. 2002. *Gender and Conflict Early-Warning: A Framework for Action.* Geneva and London: Swiss Peace Foundation and International Alert.

Sheckler, A. 2002. Why Gender Matters When the Dust Settles. *Developing Alternatives,* Vol. 8, No. (1):, pp. 27–32.

Shikola, T. 1998. We Left Our Shoes Behind. In *What Women do in Wartime: Gender and Conflict in Africa,* eds. M. Turshen and C. Twagiramariya, 138–149. London: Zed Books.

SIDA. 1998. *Conflict, Peace Building, Disarmament, Security: The Police and Equality between Women and Men.* Prepared by J. Chalky and B. Woroniuk. Stockholm: SIDA.

———. 2000. *Toward Gender Equality in Mozambique: A Profile of Gender Relations.* Stockholm: SIDA.

Sideris, T. 2000. Rape in War and Peace: Some Thoughts on Social Context and Gender Roles. *Agenda* 43: 41–45.

Sikoska, T., and J. Solomon. 2002. *Introducing Gender in Conflict and Conflict Prevention: Conceptual and Policy Implications.* Geneva: INSTRAW.

Slapsak, S. 2001. The Use of Women and the Role of Women in the Yugoslav War. In *Gender, Peace and Conflict,* eds. I. Skjelsbaek and D. Smith, 161–183. London: Sage.

Social Development Department. 1995. Gender Issues in Participation. Social Development Notes, Note No. 12, June. Washington, DC: World Bank.

———. 2003. Social Analysis Sourcebook: Incorporating Social Dimensions into Bank-Supported Projects. Washington, DC: World Bank.

Sogge, D. 1992. Sustainable Peace: Angola's Recovery. Harare: SARDC.

Sommers, M. 2002. Children, Education and War: Reaching Education for All (EFA) Objectives in Countries Affected by Conflict. Conflict Prevention and Reconstruction Unit Working Papers, No. 1, World Bank, Washington, DC.

———. 2003. Urbanization, War, and Africa's Youth at Risk, CARE Inc. and Creative Associates International Inc. Washington, DC: USAID.

Sörensen, B. 1998. Women and Post-Conflict Reconstruction: Issues and Sources, Occasional Paper 3. UNRISD/The War-Torn Societies Project. UNRISD, Geneva.

Specht, I. 2003. Jobs for Rebels and Soldiers. Chapter 4 in E. Date-Bah, Jobs after War: A Critical Challenge in the Peace and Reconstruction Puzzle. Geneva: ILO.

SP GTF (Gender Task Force of the Stability Pact for Southeastern Europe). 2002. Building National Gender Equality Mechanisms in Southeast Europe: Women's Use of the State, 1999–2001. Ljubljana: SP GTF.

Strand, A., H. Toje, A. M. Jerve, and I. Samset. 2003. Community Driven Development in Contexts of Conflict. Concept Paper Commissioned by ESSD, World Bank, Chr. Michelsen Institute, Bergen, Norway.

Strickland, R., and N. Duvvury. 2003. Gender Equity and Peace Building: From Rhetoric to Reality. Finding the Way. Discussion Paper, ICRW, Washington, DC.

Tienhoven, H. van. 1992. Sexual Violence: A Method of Torture Also Used against Male Victims. Nordisk Sexologi 1992 (10): 243–249.

———. 1993. Sexual Torture of Male Victims. Torture 3(4): 133–135.

Toure, A. 2002. The Role of Civil Society in National Reconciliation and Peace Building in Liberia. New York: International Peace Academy.

Turner, S. 1999. Angry Young Men in Camps: Gender, Age and Class Relations among Burundian Refugees in Tanzania. UNHCR Working Paper 9, UNHCR, Geneva.

Turshen, M. 1998. Women's War Stories. In What Women Do in Wartime: Gender and Conflict in Africa, eds. M. Turshen and C. Twagiramariya, London: Zed Books.

———. 2001. Engendering Relations of State to Society in the Aftermath. In The Aftermath: Women in Post-Conflict Transformation, eds. S. Meintjes, A. Pillay, and M. Turshen, 78–96. New York: Zed Books.

Turshen, M., and C. Twagiramariya, eds. 1998. What Women Do in Wartime: Gender and Conflict in Africa. London: Zed Books.

———. 1998a. Favors to Give and Consenting Victims: The Sexual Politics of Survival in Rwanda. In *What Women Do in Wartime: Gender and Conflict in Africa,* eds. M. Turshen and C. Twagiramariya, 101–117. London: Zed Books.

UN (United Nations). 2002. Women, Peace and Security: Study submitted by the Secretary-General pursuant to Security Council Resolution 1325 (2000). United Nations, New York.

UNCHS (UN Center for Human Settlements). 1999. Women's Rights to Land, Housing and Poverty in Post-Conflict Situations and During Reconstruction: A Global Overview. A Research Study Conducted with the Support of the Government of Sweden, working paper, UNCHS, Nairobi.

UNDDA (UN Department for Disarmament Affairs). 2001. *Gender Perspectives on Disarmament, Demobilization and Reintegration (DDR).* New York: DDA.

———. 2003. Department for Disarmament Affairs: Gender Mainstreaming Action Plan. DDA, New York.

UNDESA (UN Department of Economic and Social Affairs). 2001. Widowhood: Invisible Women, Secluded or Excluded. *Women 2000.* United Nations: Division for the Advancement of Women.

UNDP (UN Development Programme). 2000. *Women's Political Participation and Good Governance: Twenty-First Century Challenges.* New York: UNDP.

———. 2003. *Gender Approaches in Conflict and Post-Conflict Situations.* New York: UNDP.

UNDP/Gender in Development Program. 2001. *Learning and Information Pack: Gender Analysis.* New York: UNDP.

UNDPKO (UN Department for Peacekeeping Operations). 2000. *Mainstreaming a Gender Perspective in Multidimensional Peace Operations.* New York: Lessons Learned Unit, DPKO.

———. 2003. Handbook for Multidimensional Peacekeeping. Working paper, DPKO, New York.

UNDP/UNIFEM. 2002. Overview of Assessment and Evaluation Findings Related to Women's Rights, Gender Equality and Social Justice in Post-Conflict Rwanda. Briefing Paper 2.

UNESC (UN Economic and Social Council). 1997. Agreed Conclusions 1997/2.

UNFPA (UN Fund for Population Activities). 2002. *The Impact of Conflict on Women and Girls: A UNFPA Strategy for Gender Mainstreaming in Areas of Conflict and Reconstruction.* Bratislava: UNFPA.

UNHCR (UN High Commissioner for Refugees). 2001. *UNHCR Good Practices on Gender Equality Mainstreaming. A Practical Guide to Empowerment.* Geneva: UNHCR.

———. 2003. *Sexual and Gender-Based Violence against Refugees, Returnees and Internally Displaced Persons: Guidelines for the Preventions and Responses.* Geneva: UNHCR.

UNICEF/UNOHCHR/OSCE-ODIHR. 2002. *Trafficking in Human Beings in Southeastern Europe: Current Situation and Responses to Trafficking in Human Beings.* Belgrade: UNICEF Area Office for the Balkans.

UNIFEM (UN Development Fund for Women). 1998. *Bringing Equality Home: Implementing the Convention on the Elimination of All Forms of Discrimination Against Women (CEDAW).* New York: UNIFEM.

———. 2001. Women's Land and Property Rights in Situations of Conflict and Reconstruction: A Reader based on the February 1998 Inter-Regional Consultation in Kigali, Rwanda. UNIFEM, New York.

———. 2001a. *Picturing a Life Free of Violence: Media and Communications Strategies to End Violence against Women.* New York: UNIFEM.

United Nations Secretary-General. 2001. *Report of the Secretary-General to the Security Council on the Protection of Civilians in Armed Conflict (S/2001/331).*

UNSC (UN Security Council). 2000. *Resolution 1325 adopted by the Security Council at its 4213th Meeting, 31 October 2000. S/RES/1325(2000).*

Urdang, S. 1979. *Fighting Two Colonialisms: Women in Guinea-Bissau.* New York and London: Monthly Review Press.

USAID (United States Agency for International Development). 2000. *Women 2000, Beijing Plus Five: The USAID Commitment.* Washington, DC: USAID.

———. 2001. Aftermath: Women and Women's Organizations in Postconflict Societies. *Evaluation Highlights*, No. 74, July.

Vann, B. 2002. Gender-Based Violence: Emerging Issues in Programs Serving Displaced Populations. Reproductive Health for Refugees Consortium, c/o JSI Research and Training Institute, Arlington, VA.

Verhey, B. 2001. Child Soldiers: Preventing, Demobilizing and Reintegrating. Africa Region Working Paper Series, No. 23, World Bank, Washington, DC.

Vincent, L. 2001. Engendering Peace in Africa: A Critical Inquiry into Some Current Thinking on the Role of African Women in Peace Building. *Africa Journal for Conflict Resolution* 2001 (1).

Walsh, M. 1997. *Post-Conflict Bosnia and Herzegovina: Integrating Woman's Special Situation and Gender Perspectives in Skills' Training and Employment Promotion Programs.* Geneva: ILO.

———. 2001. Profile: Bosnia and Herzegovina. In *Women and Civil War: Impact, Organizations and Action*, ed. K. Kumar, 57–67. Boulder, Colo., and London: Lynne Rienner.

Ward, J. 2002. *If Not Now, When? Addressing Gender-Based Violence in Refugee, Internally Displaced and Post-Conflict Settings: A Global*

Overview. New York: Reproductive Health Consortium, c/o Women's Commission for Refugee Women and Children, and the International Rescue Committee.

War Report. 1995. *Women's Issues.* London: Institute for War and Peace Reporting.

War-Torn Societies Project. *Rebuilding after War: Lessons from WSP.* www.wsp-international.org/rebuilding/rebu-02.htm.

Watson, C. 1996. *The Flight, Exile and Return of Chadian Refugees: A Case Study with a Special Focus on Women.* Geneva: UNRISD.

de Watteville, N. 2002. Addressing Gender Issues in Demobilization and Reintegration Programs. Africa Region Working Papers Series, World Bank, Washington, DC.

WCRWC (Women's Commission for Refugee Women and Children). 2001. *You Cannot Dance If You Cannot Stand: A Review of the Rwanda Women's Initiative and the United Nations High Commissioner for Refugees' Commitment to Gender Equality in Post-Conflict Societies.* New York: WCRWC.

————. 2002. *Precious Resources: Adolescents in the Reconstruction of Sierra Leone.* New York: WCRWC.

Weill, C. 2003. A Hierarchy of Protection? Intrastate Conflicts and the Role of Women. International Women's Day presentation at the Embassy of the Republic of South Africa, Washington, DC, March 2003.

Weiss Fagen, P., and S. W. Yudelman. 2001. El Salvador and Guatemala: Refugee Camp and Repatriation Experiences. In *Women and Civil War: Impact, Organizations and Action,* ed. K. Kumar. Boulder, CO and London: Lynne Rienner.

WHO (World Health Organization). 1996. *Mental Health of Refugees.* Geneva: World Health Organization.

————. 2000. *Reproductive Health during Conflict and Displacement.* Geneva: World Health Organization.

————. 2001. *Gender and Reproductive Rights: Considerations for Formulating Reproductive Health Laws.* Geneva: World Health Organization.

WHO/UNFPA/UNHCR. 1999. *Reproductive Health in Refugee Situations: An Inter-Agency Field Manual.* Geneva: UNHCR.

WHO/UNHCR. 2002. *Clinical Management of Survivors of Rape: A Guide to the Development of Protocols for Use in Refugee and Internally Displaced Person Situations.* Geneva: WHO and UNHCR.

Wilford, R., and R. L. Miller, eds. 1998. *Women, Ethnicity and Nationalism: The Politics of Transition.* London: Routledge.

Wilson, A. 1991. *Women and the Eritrean Revolution: The Challenge Road.* Trenton, NJ: Red Sea Press.

Women Building Peace. 2001. *Mainstreaming Gender in Peace Building: A Framework for Action.* London: International Alert.

Women in Black. 1994. We Are (pamphlet). Women for Peace, Belgrade.

Wong, S. 2002. Do Women Make a Difference? KDP1 Gender Data Analysis Interim Report. Working paper, World Bank, Washington, DC.

Worby, P. 2001. Organizing for a Change: Guatemalan Refugee Women Reaffirm their Right to Land. Background paper in UNIFEM, *Women's Land and Property Rights in Situations of Conflict and Reconstruction: A Reader based on the February 1998 Inter-Regional Consultation in Kigali, Rwanda.* New York: UNIFEM.

World Bank. 2001. *Development Cooperation and Conflict: OP 2.30.* Washington, DC: World Bank.

———. 2001a. *Development Cooperation and Conflict: Bank Procedures BP 2.30.* Washington, DC: World Bank.

———. 2001b. *Engendering Development through Gender Equality in Rights, Resources and Voice: Summary.* Washington, DC: World Bank.

———. 2002. *Integrating Gender into the World Bank's Work: A Strategy for Action.* Washington, DC: World Bank.

———. 2003. *Development Cooperation and Conflict: Update on Implementation of OP/BP 2.30.* Washington, DC: World Bank.

———. 2003a. *Gender and Development: OP 4.20.* Washington, DC: World Bank.

———. 2003b. *Sierra Leone: Strategic Country Gender Assessment.* Washington, DC: World Bank.

———. 2004. *Afghanistan: State Building, Sustaining Growth, and Reducing Poverty.* Working paper, Poverty Reduction and Economic Management Sector Unit, South Asia Region (June). World Bank, Washington, DC.

World Bank Jakarta/PPK (Program Pengembangan Kecamatan). 2003. *Enhancing Women's Participation: Learning from Field Experience.* Jakarta: World Bank.

Woroniuk, B. 2001. *Gender Equality and Peace Building: Operational Framework.* Washington DC: Conflict Prevention and Post-Conflict Reconstruction (CPR) Network.

Zimbabwe Women Writers. 2000. *Women of Resilience: The Voices of Women Combatants.* London and Harare: African Books Collective.

Zuckerman, E., and M. E. Greenberg. 2004. The Gender Dimensions of Post-Conflict Reconstruction. Paper presented at the June 2004 UNU-WIDER Conference Making Peace Work in Helsinki.

Index

Boxes and tables are indicated by b and t respectively.

Printed in the United States
99839LV00004B/1-72/A